FOLK DRUMMING IN THE HIMALAYAS

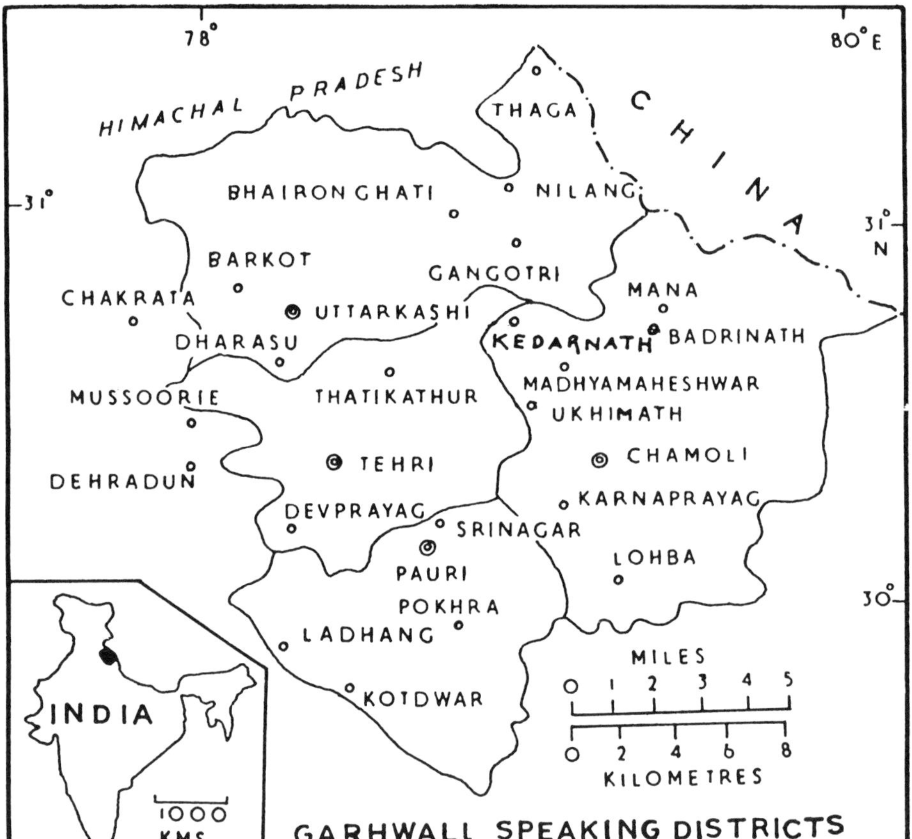

GARHWALI SPEAKING DISTRICTS

FOLK DRUMMING IN THE HIMALAYAS

A Linguistic Approach to Music

by
Anoop Chandola

AMS PRESS, INC.
New York

FIRST AMS PRESS EDITION: 1977

Library of Congress Cataloguing in Publication Data
Main entry under author

Chandola, Anoop.
Folk drumming in the Himalayas.

Bibliography: p.
1. Folk music—Garhwal, India (District)—History
and criticism. 2. Garhwali dialect. 3. Folk-songs,
Garhwali-History and criticism. I. Title.
ML3748.C52 789'.1 76-23549
ISBN: 0-404-15403-4
LIBRARY OF CONGRESS CATALOG CARD NUMBER 76-23549

We gratefully acknowledge permission to quote from
Alan P. Merriam's *The Anthropology of Music*, published
by Northwestern University Press.

PREFACE

Music has not yet received its due place in the social sciences. It is usually studied and taught as a fine art, while in fact it is important not so much as a practice in esthetics as in a therapeutic way. In the Himalayan culture, for example, music has auspicious, shamanistic and recreational functions which are overtly or covertly therapeutic in nature. These functions aim at the fulfillment of various kinds of physical, spiritual and psychological needs of the members participating in the culture and society. Because such needs are related to various behavioral patterns, a single discipline cannot encompass them all. In order to understand the complete nature and scope of music, an interdisciplinary approach is needed.

Regardless of the approach used for the study of music, it is a fact that music, like language, is a sign system. The basic signs of music are its tonal and rhythmic markers. Musicology and linguistics have developed sophisticated theories and methods by which to study the sign systems of music and language, respectively. In addition to the shared characteristic of both being sign systems, music and language have another element in common in that they both can be expressed in sound. Although each has its own system of sounds, the two are united in singing, which is both a linguistic and a musical utterance. Singing can also be accompanied by musical instruments, thus adding another aspect to the diversity of the subject of music. Because of these factors, an interdisciplinary field, which we will call musicolinguistics, would obviously be a useful addition to the study of music.

One of my two major aims in this work is to demonstrate how linguistic concepts can be applied to the study of music. For this purpose I have chosen the Indian folk music of the Himalayas as it is found in the Garhwali speaking area. This rich folk tradition has not previously received any scientific attention. Because of the tremendous socio-political changes which India has experienced in the past few decades, and which it will continue to experience, this folk tradition is destined to die by the end of the century. Therefore, the second major aim of this work is to prevent the academic 'melting away' of this Himalayan tradition.

This work is primarily addressed to linguists, folklorists, ethnomusicologists, and anthropologists; but it should also be of general interest to all those concerned with Indian and Himalayan studies.

Musicolinguistic studies of a limited nature have existed since pre-Christian times. For example, the Indic phoneticians discussed musical tones in connection with the accentual system of Vedic or Sanskrit in the *Pāṇinīyaśikṣā,* supposedly authored by Pāṇini, the author of the famous Sanskrit grammar, the *Aṣṭādhyāyī* (ca. 400 B.C.). Recently, a few small but inspiring studies have been made, notably articles by Springer (1956), Chao (1956), Nettl (1958), Bright (1963), and Austerlitz (1966, 1967). (See also articles by Chandola 1969, 1970, and others.) Since these articles are limited in scope, a more detailed study was felt necessary which would include consideration of musical instruments as well as the more limited subject of the interaction of music and language. The suitability of the interaction of music and language in a song text as a subject for linguistic study is fairly obvious. In comparison, the application of linguistics to drums and their sound patterns may seem at first to be both unusual and unworkable. However, as this work seeks to demonstrate, any musical instrument and its music can be described by the methods used by linguists to describe language. The present work is a first step in this direction and should be considered a beginning effort to develop the study of musicolinguistics. It is hoped that it will serve as a point of departure for more intensive and extensive research, comparable to that which we see in other interdisciplinary approaches, such as is exemplified by works like Carl E. Seashore's *Psychology of Music* and Alexander Wood's *The Physics of Music.*

Although my interest in Himalayan folklore led me to make Himalayan efforts in the field, or rather, in the high mountains of the Garhwali region, during the course of the 1973-74 academic year, at times causing discomfort to my family members as well as myself, it now gives me nothing but pleasure to be able to help preserve this dying Himalayan tradition for the academic world.

The present work has been supported by the National Science Foundation whose Anthropology Program gave a grant (No. GS-39703) for my project 'An Ethnomusicolinguistic Study of the Folk Mahabharata Drumming in a Himalayan Culture'. Under this project I did field work during the academic year 1973-74 with research leave from the University of Arizona.

In completing this project I had an opportunity to work with so many people that it is not possible for me to express my gratitude to all of them in this limited space. I would like, however, to mention some of those whose participation has left clear marks on this work.

In analyzing the drumming, I was helped by Shyam Sundar Srivastava and Vijay Krishan. Most of the song texts were prepared by Keshav Anuragi. Some were prepared by Vijay Johri and Madan Mohan Joshi. I am most grateful to these classical musicians and musicologists.

The Garhwali folk artists whose performance is the subject of this work are listed here as teams, along with their musical instruments: Bhardas and Dulbudas for the Dhol and Damau; Bachandas and Dipudas for the Dhol and Damau; Kundan and his wife Bijli for the Dholki and dance with Ghungrus; Saphri and his wife Janki for the Dholki and dance with Ghungrus; Bansi for the Daunr and Hurki, assisted by Khusal on the Thali with horn, and by Sohan on the Thali with sticks; Janardan for the Daunr and Hurki, assisted by Sib Chand and Diwan Singh on the Thali with sticks. I am emotionally overwhelmed whenever I hear the tapes of their performances. These folk artists have very little of what we call material possessions, but they have offered me their most cherished wealth — their Himalayan folk music. I will always owe them a Himalayan debt of gratitude for this.

It was due to the efforts of my father that these folk artists were available. He, aided by the advice of my mother and also my mother-in-law and father-in-law, located and persuaded the best artists to join us. They all, therefore, certainly deserve my deepest respect and gratitude.

The photographs of the musical instruments showing the stroke positions were taken by Brahm Dev, for which he deserves my sincere thanks.

My previous research in musicolinguistics has received comments from several linguists, ethnomusicologists and anthropologists. I have considered and benefited from their suggestions in the present work. Among them I wish to thank especially Robert Austerlitz, Naomi Owens, Rodney Mercado, Edgar Polome, and Paul Turner.

Major credit goes to Linda Wentink in the final preparation of the manuscript of this work, for which I am extremely thankful to her. I want to thank also Evelyn Varaday for her initial help in the manuscript preparation. For the map of Garhwali-speaking districts, I am indebted to A.K. Tiwari, Professor of Geography, Jodhpur University.

This manuscript was read by two linguists — Shaligram Shukla and Fr. Richard O'Brien. I am very grateful to them for their highly valuable comments and suggestions.

I must thank Sudha who, not only as a wife, but also as a scholar, worked hard with me in order to bring this project to a successful conclusion.

Finally, I will be most appreciative of and thankful to those who read this work and bring to my notice their comments and suggestions.

CONTENTS

I THE ETHNOMUSICOLINGUISTIC BACKGROUND AND FIELD METHODOLOGY

Location, Language, and Music ... 1
Social Stratification ... 4
Musicians' Physical Appearance ... 6
The Functional Aspects of Drumming ... 7
Dancing and Drumming ... 13
The Learning of Drumming ... 15
The *Mahābhārata* Folklore ... 18
Field Methodology ... 21

II THE PHONETIC MECHANISM

General Remarks ... 27
The Dhol ... 29
The Damau ... 30
The Dholki ... 31
The Ghungrus ... 32
The Daunr ... 32
The Pathu ... 33
The Thali ... 33
The Thali Horn and Sticks ... 33
The Hurki ... 34

III THE PHONETIC DESCRIPTION OF THE STROKES ....

General Remarks 35
The Dhol Sounds 39
The Damau Sounds 41
The Dholki Sounds 41
The Ghungru Sounds 43
The Daunr Sounds 43
The Thali-Pathu Sounds 44
The Hurki Sounds 45
The Thali-Stick Sounds 46

IV DISTRIBUTIONAL PATTERNS OF SOUNDS ....

General Remarks 47
The Distribution of the Dhol-Damau Strokes 50
The Distribution of the Dholki-Ghungru Strokes 54
The Distribution of the Daunr-Thali Strokes 57
The Distribution of the Hurki-Thali Strokes 59

V TEXTUAL ASPECTS ....

Song texts and the Singers 61
Textual Variation 66
Linguistic Abnormalities 71
Meter 76
Final Remarks 79

ILLUSTRATIONS 81

APPENDIX 85

Dhol Text 1 87
Language Text of Dhol Text 1 95
Dhol Text 2 98
Language Text of Dhol Text 2 102
Dhol Text 3 (no drums) 104
Language Text of Dhol Text 3 108
Dhol Text 4 (Prosaic—Non-Musical) 110
Dhol Text 5 112
Language Text of Dhol Text 5 116
Dhol Text 6 (Prosaic—Non-Musical) 118
Dholki Text 1 119
Language Text of Dholki Text 1 120
Language Text of Dholki Text 2 120
Dholki Text 3 121
Language Text of Dholki Text 3 123
Dholki Text 4 125
Language Text of Dholki Text 4 127
Daunr Text 1 129
Language Text of Daunr Text 1 131
Daunr Text 2 134
Language Text of Daunr Text 2 136
Hurki Text 1 137
Language Text of Hurki Text 1 140
Hurki Text 2 142
Language Text of Hurki Text 2 145
A *ghasyari* Song Text 146
Language Text of the *ghasyari* Song Text 148
mā̃gal Text 149
Language Text of the *mā̃gal* Text 151

BIBLIOGRAPHY 153

I

ETHNOMUSICOLINGUISTIC BACKGROUND AND FIELD METHODOLOGY

Location, Language, and Music

The area to be examined in this musicolinguistic study is that region where Garhwali is spoken today. This area, known also as the Garhwal Himalayas, is one of the two subgroups of the Pahari Himalayas. The term *Garhwal*, pronounced in Garhwali as *gáḍwāl*, and in Hindi as *gaṛhwāl*, means 'the region of forts'. It is said that the rajas of Garhwal had many fortresses or *gáḍ*; *wāḷ* is a possessive suffix, hence the name *gáḍwāl*. The adjective or nominal suffix *i* is attached to *gáḍwāl*, making it *gaḍwāḷi* (Hindi *gaṛhwālī*), meaning 'belonging to Garhwal, the Garhwali language'. The words 'Garhwal' or 'Garhwali' are the anglicized spellings which reflect the Hindi writing and pronunciation. The word *Himalaya* is made up of two Sanskrit words, *hima* 'snow' and *ālaya* 'abode'. In addition, the term *Pahari* (Hindi *pahāṛī*, Garhwali *pā́ṛi*) means 'hill, hill man, hilly'. The Pahari region, encompassing the world's highest elevations, is situated between Tibet in the north, Nepal in the east, the Indo-Gangetic plains in the south, and Kashmir in the west.

The linguistic development of the Pahari languages is the subject of very few studies. Works by Grierson (1916), Chatterjee (1938), and Turner (1931) are still the main sources for understanding the evolution and distribution of the Pahari languages. In general, however, the Pahari languages may be viewed as being divided into three areas: Eastern Pahari, containing Nepali and its various dialects; Western Pahari, including languages such as Jaunsari (spoken in the Jaunsar region of Dehradun in Uttar Pradesh), and

Mandiyali (spoken in Himachal Pradesh) and Central Pahari, divided into two languages, Kumaoni and Garhwali. Thus, the linguistic focal point of this study, Garhwali, is a Central Pahari language which, in turn, is a branch of the New Indo-Aryan languages.

Surrounded by Tibetan in the north, Kumaoni in the east, Khari Boli Hindi in the south, and Jaunsari in the west, Garhwali is widely spoken in the four Himalayan districts of U.P. (despite the fact that Hindi-Urdu is the official language of the entire Garhwali speaking area). These districts — Pauri Garhwal, Tehri Garhwal, Chamoli, and Uttar Kashi — are mostly rural. Nevertheless, within them there are about a dozen Garhwali speaking population centers classified as towns, such as Pauri, Shrinagar, Tehri, Narendranagar, Rishikesh, Lansdown, Kotdwar, Karnprayag, Joshimath, Dugadda, etc. (In the northern region, around Badrinath, Kedarnath, Niti, and Mana, the people of Tibetan stock speak Marchhyali, a Tibeto-Burman language. However, they can speak or understand Garhwali.) In addition to the town populations of the four Himalayan districts cited above, the majority of the inhabitants of the cities of Mussoorie and Dehradun speak Garhwali. Furthermore, there are Garhwali speakers in all the major cities of U.P. (Lucknow, Merath, Agra, Allahabad, Varanasi, etc.), and a sizeable number in Delhi, as well.

Like Hindi and Sanskrit, Garhwali is written in the Devanagari script. However, despite the fact that the Garhwali region has produced scholars of national fame, Garhwali, unlike Hindi and Sanskrit, has no literary history. In this century, some efforts have been made to make Garhwali a literary language, but so far, it has not achieved that status. Garhwali is not an official or educational language at any level (Hindi is the language for these functions). Even illiterate Garhwali speakers, with a few exceptions, speak or understand Hindi-Urdu. The scope of Garhwali will continue to decrease.

The notational system for Garhwali language sounds, adopted in this work, is based upon the International Romanization of Sanskrit sounds. Listed below, in the phonetic order of Devanagari, are the sounds of Garhwali in Romanized letters.

Vowels: a, ā, i, ī, u, ū, e, ē, ai, o, ō, au

Consonants: k, kh, g, gh, n̄, c, ch, j, jh, ṭ, ṭh, ḍ, ṛ, ḍh, ṇ, t, th, d, dh, n, p, ph, b, bh, m, y, r, ḷ, l, lh, w, s, h

Nasalization ˜, Circumflex tone ´.

The long vowels *ai* and *au* represent the phonetic value of [æ] and [ɔ] respectively. The sound *r* is a voiced flap consonant. The consonant *ḷ* is a dental flap retroflex, a unique sound in the Indo-

European languages. The sound *s* may vary freely with *ś* in some dialects. In addition, a vowel may be nasalized; e.g. *ā̃* is a long nasalized vowel. The circumflex tone first rises and then falls on the vowel of a monosyllabic word: e.g. *bṓl* 'speak!' is [bō̂l] as contrasted with *bol* 'speech'. In a polysyllabic word, the circumflex tone is distributed over two vowels. The first has the rising tone and following has the falling tone: e.g. *cṓḷa* 'apricot' is [cṓḷà] as contrasted with *cōḷa* 'gown'. The vowels without the circumflex tone have an even tone. These linguistic tones do not influence the musical tones in any way. The tone may be considered as a variant of *h* after a vowel if one follows the complementary distribution method as developed in Bloomfield (1933), Block and Trager (1942), Pike (1947), and Harris (1951). However, I have determined that the above mentioned tone is different from *h* since the impressions are different to the hearer. (For the impressionistic criterion, see Chandola 1969.)

The notation of the octave tones of Garhwali singing employs the Romanization of the Indian octave tones. These twelve tones — C, D♭, D, E♭, E, F, F♯, G, A♭, A, B♭, B — correspond to the Hindustani (North Indian) octave tones which are respectively as follows: sa, re♭, re, ga♭, ga, ma, ma♯, pa, dha♭, dha, ni♭, ni. The texts have been presented in the former alphabetic system according to the Indian convention. Other specific details pertaining to the notational system will appear in the chapter entitled 'Textual Aspects'. Furthermore, in order to parallel the tonal notation, an alphabetic system has been adopted to represent the drum strokes. The symbols for the strokes of each drum will be discussed in successive chapters.

It should be noted here that the octave notation is simply an analytic device adopted by the trained musicians and the musicologists who worked with me. Folksingers are unaware of this octave system; rather than employing a written notational system, they sing impressionistically. Moreover, it has been demonstrated by Jairazbhoy and Stone (1963) that in actual performance, musicians overlap widely in the range of frequencies of the octave tones. Thus, similar to the folksinger, the musician, in an impressionistic manner, simply adopts the tonal frequencies utilized by his teachers. The notational conventions of North Indian classical music's octave tones and frequencies (including rhythmic notations) are established in Bhatkande's works.

The musical performers, observed as part of this study, tend to be teamed together according to their instruments as follows: Dhol-Damau, Dholki-Ghungru, Daunr-Thali, and Hurki-Thali. (In Garwali these instruments are pronounced in the following manner: *dhōl-damāu*, *ḍholki-ghuñgru*, *ḍāur-thāḷi*, and *huṛki-thāḷi*.) With the exception of the female dancer-singer who wears the Ghungru 'ankle bells', all the musicians are male, and all of them, including the Ghungru dancer, are singers as well. Each of the four groups contains drummers. In addition, the Daunr and the Hurki, both small drums, are accompanied by the Thali 'plate or dish' used as a drum. Although the Ghungru and Thali are not structurally drums, they serve the same function. More details about each instrument and their sound systems will appear in the proceeding chapters.

Social Stratification

Isolated from its social environment, music cannot be fully understood. As Merriam (1964) aptly said, "Music cannot be defined as a phenomenon of sound alone; for it involves the behavior of individuals and groups of individuals; its particular organization demands the social concurrence of people who decide what it can and cannot be." For this reason, the sociocultural context of Garhwali drumming will be described within various sections in the remainder of this chapter.

Garhwali Hindus, comprising a subgroup of Pahari society, are traditionally divided into two major classes; *bit* and *ḍūm*. The term *biṭ* refers to the traditional castes called *dviṭ* or *dvija*, 'twice born' in Sanskrit, while the word *ḍūm* represents the Sanskrit *ḍoma*, 'untouchable'. At present, the word *ḍūm* (or *ḍōm*) is considered to be highly derogatory, and its use is punishable according to Indian law. The more acceptable expression employed by Garhwalis is *silpkār* or *silipkār* 'artisan' (from Sanskrit *śilpakāra*). (Gandhi's euphemism *harijan* 'God's people', is not commonly used in the Garhwali region.)

The sector of Garhwali Hindus known as *biṭ* comprises two major subgroups: *bā́maṇ*, Sanskrit *brāhmaṇa*, 'priest'; and *jajmān*, Sanskrit *yajamāna*, 'doer of the *yajña*' or 'client'. Traditionally, *bā́maṇ* 'brahmin', represents the priestly class, and the *jajmān* consists of the *kṣatriya*, 'protector, warrior' class.

There are other names by which these groups are known. *Rajpūt* (Sanskrit *Rājaputra* 'royal descendant') or *Khasya* (Sanskrit *khaśa*) are also employed in reference to the *jajmān* class. Since *khasya* is considered to indicate an inferior Rajput class, some *jajman* prefer to be called *ṭhākur*.

The traditional third class, *vaiśya* 'businessman' is barely perceptible in Garhwali society. They comprise a very small minority, mostly recent settlers. Thus, of the four major customary *varṇa* 'groups', namely *brāhmaṇa*, *kṣatriya*, *vaiśya*, and *śūdra*, basically only three are represented in Garhwali society: *bāmaṇ*, *jajmān*, and *silpkār*. Each of the above *varṇa* is further subdivided into *jāt* (Sanskrit *jāti*) 'castes'. These divisions are somewhat flexible, for example, in the Indian army, air force, navy, and police, there are members of all the major classes. Yet, there are some roles which may be fulfilled only by a particular group: e.g. a shaman may be a member of any caste, but a priest is always a Brahmin. There are similar caste requirements placed upon the musicians studied. All the drummers observed are members of *silpkār* castes; their specific *jātis*, however, vary. The Dhol-Damau players are of the *auji* caste; the Dholki-Ghungru team are of the *baddi* caste; whereas the Daunr-Thali and the Hurki-Thali musicians may be from any caste.

As members of the *jātis* mentioned above, the drummers observed in this project were not solely musicians; they had other occupations as well. For example, the Dhol-Damau players, according to tradition, were both drummers and tailors. They also did some farming and raised livestock. The women of the *auji* caste, besides helping their men in those ceremonies in which drumming is involved, did the usual household and farm work. Unlike the drummers of the other *jātis*, the *auji* musicians tended to have a fixed clientele in their own villages, or in others nearby.

Men of the *baddi* caste, as mentioned previously, play the Dholki accompanied by women who dance while wearing the Ghungru. The woman who accompanies the Dholki player is usually his wife; the young Dholki player, however, generally starts his musical career accompanied by his mother or his sister. As members of the *baddi* caste, these musicians are seminomadic; they change their domiciles more frequently than any other caste or community in this region. Although some do have a fixed clientele, most of them do not. In addition to drumming, some raise goats, sheep, and horses. (Sheep are used for wool and for meat; goats are raised for meat and for their manure; horses are used strictly for riding and for the purpose of increasing one's social prestige.) Besides raising animals, the *baddi* caste members also make combs, usually fashioned from bamboo wood.

Since the players of the Daunr-Thali and the Hurki-Thali may be members of any caste, it is difficult to generalize about their caste backgrounds. Nevertheless, it was observed that they also had more than one occupation. One team of the Daunr-Thali players, who also played the Hurki-Thali, was of the *tamoṭa* caste of the *silpkār* group. The *tamoṭa* caste members traditionally make metal containers for household use; they also do farming and raise livestock. Like the other musicians, they have some fixed clientele, but that tradition is waning. Another team of musicians who played Daunr-Thali and Hurki-Thali belonged to the *lwār* caste whose customary occupation is that of the blacksmith. However, these drummers of the *lwār* caste whom I observed were also doing plumbing, masonry, road construction, farming, and were raising livestock.

There are additional terms, not as yet mentioned, by which these musicians are known. The Dhol player is referred to as *ḍholya* or *ḍholi dās*; the Damau player is called *damaiyā̃*; and the common term for both players is *dās*. The word *dās* has lost its etymological meaning which is 'slave, servant, serf'. In reference to the Dhol-Damau players, the word *dās* means 'master or devotee' of the drums. Moreover, *dās* is employed as an honorific address to the Dhol-Damau drummers. Another name used in reference to these drummers is *bajgi*. Like the name of his caste, the Dholki drummer is called *baddi* and sometimes *ḍholkya*; the dancer who accompanies him is known as *badīn* or *badini*. Moreover, the common term for the Daunr-Thali or Hurki-Thali players is *dhāmi*. There is no separate name for the Thali player; yet, the Daunr player and the Hurki player are known separately as *ḍaũrya* and *huṛkya* respectively.

Musicians' Physical Appearance

The physical differences of the *silpkār* and the *non-silpkār* castes of the Garhwali region have been pointed out in the anthropological study of Majumdar (1944). However, the physical features ascribed to the *silpkārs* by Majumdar may also be seen in the *bit* castes, and vice versa. (Berreman 1963 reinforces this viewpoint.) As noted by the historians Grierson (1916), Raturi (1928), and Sankrityan (1958), it seems that as a result of the historical movement of various ethnic groups in the Himalayas ethnic mergers occurred. Thus, the outgrowth of these mergers is the general ethnic group known as *pahāṛī*, 'hill man'. A typical *pahāṛi* of this region has Aryan (Caucasian) features with Mongol (Tibetan) and Dravidian types. Similarly, the physical appearance of the musicians studied may also be considered, ethnically, *pahāṛī*.

Like their features, the attire of the male *pahāṛī* musicians is a combination of various features. They wear Indian style *pajama* 'pants' (loose or tight), *kurta* 'long shirts', and hill style collarless jackets and long coats. On their heads, they wear either *ṭopi* 'caps' or turbans. However, traditional men's apparel is being replaced by western style jackets, shirts, and pants. Thus at present, standard Indian, western and indigenous hill style clothing are all worn by men in the Garhwali region. As to whether or not they shave, that varies among individuals. However, most of the men of the baddi caste do not shave, in accordance with their belief that Lord Śiva asked them to refrain from shaving. However, schoolboys and some adult men, who have abandoned Dhokli playing, do cut their hair.

As for women of the Garhwali region, their dress is more traditional. Most wear *sāṛī* 'sarees'; but a few dress in the *ghagru* (or *ghagri*) which are long wide skirts. The upper garments for women are hill style blouses which are long sleeved and longer than the standard Indian style. The women also wear many ornaments. Earrings, gold or silver nose rings in different sizes and shapes, ankle bracelets, toe rings, necklaces, bangles, and lockets are generally worn. (However, widows do not wear nose rings or bangles. These are removed at the time of their husband's death.) An additional adornment, the colored spot on the forehead, *bindi*, is used as a cosmetic by married and unmarried women, but forbidden for widows. Although men have their ears pierced, they usually do not wear earrings, nor do they tend to wear jewelry.

The Garhwali culture is experiencing many sharp changes. As previously mentioned, traditional attire is often replaced by western style clothing. Although women have not changed their manner of dress very much, they have begun to adopt western cosmetics. For example, one dancer was seen using Pond's cream and talcum powder on her face.

The Functional Aspects of Drumming

Drumming is the main musical form of artistic expression in Garhwali culture. However, drumming is not essential to all types of Garhwali folk music. There are certain song texts which are performed entirely without drumming — for example, the *māgaḷ* 'benediction songs'. These are usually sung by women at ceremonious occasions, such as the time at which a sacred bath is given to a bride or groom, at the reception or leave-taking of the bridegroom's party, and during other rites such as ear piercing, investiture of the sacred thread, a male's first haircut, etc. Children's songs, group dance songs such as the *cǎuphḷu*, and songs recently popularized, or those dealing with contemporary themes, may be sung by anyone without drumming. Both men and women can sing such contemporary songs, either individually or together. Men and women often sing together, especially on occasions such as a group dance like the *cãuphḷu*. Contemporary songs mostly deal with situations of romance, humor, social injustice and reforms, martial themes, and special events. However, since our main concern here is drumming, the above types of songs will be excluded.

The social role of the musical instruments may be viewed as having three types of functions: auspicious, shamanistic, and recreational. The term 'auspicious' refers to the following types of occasions:

a. Rites and ceremonies (Sanskrit *samskāra*): e.g., the naming ceremony on the twelfth day after birth, the wedding ceremony, etc.
b. Religious or mythical hero worship: e.g., the *paṇḍaũ* dances based upon the *Mahābhārata* epic, and the worship of some gods and goddesses.
c. The *sãngrā̃d* (Sanskrit *saṁkrānti*) 'first day of the month' celebration.
d. The *caiti* songs sung in celebrating the new year during the first Hindu month.
e. The ceremonies for homecomings and housewarmings.
f. Any public worship or ceremony, e.g. inauguration of a temple.
g. Any traditional Hindu festival, e.g. the parade on the last day of *rāmlīla* 'the theatrical performance of the epic *Rāmāyaṇa*'.

In addition to the above, there are other 'auspicious' functions of the Dhol-Damau. After the death of an adult in the villages, the kin group observes a mourning period for the duration of one year. During the mourning period, the Dhol-Damau may not be played. At the end of the year, the Dhol-Damau musicians go to the home of the dead person's family and play the drums to mark the end of the mourning period. However, during the time of mourning the Damau may be played without the Dhol if certain obligatory ceremonies in the category of *saṁskāra* ('a' above), or the worship of important deities occurs. Furthermore, the Damau, alone, may be played in less elaborate ceremonies such as those mentioned in 'c' to 'e' above.

In all of the 'auspicious' ceremonies a Brahmin may preside, but never a shaman. Moreover, the language of the ritualistic texts, in this context, is Sanskrit. On the other hand, the shamanistic function of drumming is performed to the accompaniment of Garhwali texts. A shaman's services are required when gods, goddesses, or ghostly spirits are supposedly displeased. The gods and goddesses playing a role in the shaman's rituals are as follows: *Nirañkār* (Sanskrit *nirañkāra* 'Formless God'), *Kresn* (Sanskrit *Kṛṣṇa* 'Krishna') also called *Nāgraja* or *Nāgarja* (Sanskrit *Nāga-Rāja* 'Snake-King'), *Nársiñ* (Sanskrit *nrsiṁha* 'The Man-lion God'), *Dēbi* (Sanskrit *Devī* 'Goddess'), *Bhairāu* (Sanskrit *Bhairava* 'The Terrible God'), etc. The goddesses, *Dēbi*, are divided into several types, and there are two types of *Nársiñ*: *Dūdya* 'milky', and *Daũṇḍya* 'noisy'. Along with the above are all troublesome ghosts, both male and female. The musical instruments used to invoke, provoke, propitiate, or scare away any one of these deities or spirits are the Daunr and the Hurki; the Thali generally accompanies both.

Although all of the drums may be played for recreational purposes, some are used more frequently than others. For example, the function of the Daunr and the Hurki is predominantly shamanistic, while Dholki-Ghungru performances are always recreational. The Dholki songs are either devotional or secular. The subjects of the secular songs vary from the lives and deeds of individuals or groups to contemporary events or social problems. These songs sung by Dholki-Ghungru teams may be comic or tragic in mood. They are usually in Garhwali, but may also be sung in Hindi-Urdu (sometimes from Hindi-Urdu movie scores) and occasionally in Kumaoni or Nepali.

Another type of singing which is also recreational by nature is *pawara* 'ballad singing'. A *pawaṛa*, performed by the Hurki-Thali, recounts the story of a *bhaṛ* 'brave man' or a *rāja* 'king'. These tales are usually set in the Garhwali and Kumaoni regions. Although drumming frequently accompanies the *pawaṛa* and other recreational songs, it is not compulsory.

At times, auspicious and recreational functions may follow each other. When this occurs, only the Dhol-Damau and the Dholki-Ghungru may be present simultaneously. For example, when a wedding takes place, the Dhol-Damau are played as auspicious drums; right before or after the ceremony, the Dholki-Ghungru team may perform, but not the Hurki or Daunr. The *lāñ* 'bam- boo pole ceremony further illustrates this point. To invoke rain at times of drought or to destroy the enemies of good crops (e.g. rats), the *lāñ* ceremony is performed. During the ceremony, a Dholki player climbs to the top of a long bamboo pole, places his abdomen on the tip of the pole, and spins around. This is done to please the gods and all the communities of the area. The Dholki drummer, a *baddi* by caste, is given a holy bath before he climbs the pole. From the time of his bath until he descends the Dhol-Damau are played, because this entire duration is considered to be auspicious. Before the sacred bath there is great celebration and the Dholki-Ghungru may be performed at that time. Moreover, on the night before the *lān̄* ceremony the Dholki player and his wife may sing humorous and obscene songs (to only an adult male audience). The Daunr and the Hurki are never used either immediately before or during the *lān̄* ceremony.

Besides the instruments mentioned above, there are others which are used for recreation such as the flute, tabla, harmonium, sarangi, and Scotch bagpipes. Of these other instruments, only the tabla is a drum, but one which does not have Garhwali folk characteristics. Thus it is excluded from the present study. (A brief study of the tabla from a linguistic point of view is available in Chandola 1969.) There are other Garhwali folk instruments played for general amusement such as the *raṇsin̄ga*, or *bhaukura* and the *algoja*. (The *raṇsin̄ga* or *bhaũkura* is a horn and unable to produce a complete octave. The *algoja* is an instrument consisting of two flutes joined together which produces two octave lengths of tones.) In addition, conches, bells, cymbals, and tongs are used in devotional contexts. Since the above mentioned instruments are not regular percussion instruments with any rhythmic complexities, they are excluded from the present study.

To sum up, then, the drums observed in this study have three types of functions: auspicious, shamanistic, and recreational. Moreover, each drum has a role according to its gender. For reasons not clearly known, each drum has a nonlinguistic gender, or sex, which may differ from its linguistic gender. Neither the size nor the complexity of the stroke patterns seems to determine the nonlinguistic gender. The genders of the instruments are listed below as follows:

Instrument	Nonlinguistic Gender	Linguistic Gender
Dhol	female	masculine
Damau	male	masculine
Dholki	male	feminine
Daunr	male	masculine
Hurki	male	feminine
Thali	female	feminine

There are masculine forms of Hurki as 'huṛku' and Dholki as 'dholku', but the feminine forms are more commonly used.

Although the reason for the nonlinguistic gender of the drums is not clear, a sex linked pattern emerges. The drums which are considered to have male gender, nonlinguistically, may be played in certain contexts without the accompaniment of another drum or Thali. Thus, the Damau may be played without the Dhol, the Dholki without the Ghungru, the Daunr without the Thali, and the Hurki without the Thali. Furthermore, as was previously stated, neither the size nor the complexity of the drum strokes determines the gender. For example, the Dhol is the largest bass drum, yet it is considered to be female; the Damau is smaller than the Dhol and is high pitched, yet it is considered to be male. Moreover, the rhythmic stroke patterns of the Dhol are far more complex than those of the Damau. However, in the case of the other 'male' drums, their 'female' partners are smaller, relatively higher pitched, and less complex in their stroke patterns.

The difference in sex roles of the drums is illustrated during certain ceremonies. At some religious services, vermilion or turmeric paste is applied to the foreheads of the images of the deities and to the foreheads of all humans present. The drummers place the paste with rice on top of their drums; they offer it to the 'male' drums first. (Since Ghungrus are not considered to be drums, they do not play a part in this type of worship.)

Does Garhwali drumming have a similar communicative function to the drumming of certain native cultures of America and Africa? (See, for example, Herzog 1945 for such a study.) The answer is no. However, a set of conventions observed by the Dhol-Damau drummers is used to indicate certain kinds of information. For instance, at the time of a marriage the bridegroom's party, accompanied by a Dhol-Damau team, goes to the bride's home which is located in a different village or town. The bridegroom's group may approach the bride's home only after certain ceremonies, performed by the priest on the bride's side, have been completed (e.g. the *stambha* 'pillar' worship of the marriage altar). Upon completion of the ceremony, the priest asks the Dhol-Damau players, on the bride's side, to signal by drumming to the bridegroom's party. Awaiting this signal, the groom's Dhol-Damau players drum their response. (Certain rhythmic patterns are employed in order to communicate these signals). Then the bride's party, headed by their Dhol-Damau drummers, leaves the bride's home to receive the approaching bridegroom's assemblage, headed by their Dhol-Damau players. The drummers of both parties greet each other by beating extremely complex rhythmic patterns, turn by turn, in juxtaposition. Their encounter is filled with intensely exciting moments of artistic rivalry. Finally, the drummers exchange their partners. That is, the Dhol player of the bridegroom's party is accompanied by the Damau player of the bride's party and vice versa. Afterward, all four drummers play together. The exchange and final musical union indicate acceptance and harmony among the musicians and their respective wedding parties.

In the example of the marriage mentioned above, the drummers' distribution of rhythms and texts is fixed for each occasion. However, in other contexts, drummers have more options as to the quality and quantity of rhythms, intonations, and texts. In other situations, besides the song texts, the drummers may use spoken language intermittently, especially when communicating to a possessed person. The following example illustrates this pattern.

One morning, we were recording the *Dēbi* (or *Devī*) 'goddess' texts with the Hurki-Thali drummers. Suddenly, we discovered that despite the loud music, our cook seemed to be sleeping in a corner of the porch, and breathing heavily. We laughed, but not the drummers. The senior drummer, the Hurki player, told us that the cook was possessed. One of my brothers, who is a medical graduate with a specialty in anesthesiology, was present at the time. Although he thought that the cook was faking, my brother went to examine him. By then, with his head bent and his eyes closed, the cook was wheezing more and more heavily. My brother found that the cook's pulse was normal but his breathing pattern had become irregular. The senior drummer interrupted and told us very politely that the cook was not sick, but undoubtedly possessed. With my tape recorder still operating, I asked the senior drummer to do whatever he deemed necessary for the invocation of the spirit of *Dēbi* 'goddess'. The entire ensuing performance consisted of various rhythms which, for convenience, will be differentiated by the letters 'A', 'B', 'C', 'D'. After my request, the drummers began beating Rhythm A with a text meant for the invocation of *Dēbi*.

The musicians knew that the goddess was involved because it was during the recording of the song text of the *Dēbi* that the cook had become possessed. As the invocation continued the cook began to shake, and placed his hands, forming a bow shape, over his head. He screamed in a squeaking voice and, at times, threw his arms up into the air and turned his head around, as his eyeballs moved dizzily. In normal (spoken) language, the senior drummer asked the cook the reasons for the *Dēbi's* arrival and the location from which she had come. The cook, now the *Dēbi*, answered in abnormal intonations while screaming intermittently in squeaky tones. The answer was that the *Dēbi* had come from Tehri Garhwal and wished to protect us. (That is, my family; most of us were ill in those days.)

The drummers then changed their rhythm to B. The *Dēbi* (in the form of the cook) arose and began to dance in a frenzy; while dancing, he screamed and intermittently spoke in a semimusical intonation. At that time, my father and mother entered the room carrying rice, *urad* 'black beans' (considered sacred), vermilion paste, *ghee* 'clarified butter', and Rs. 1.25 (the Indian currency) in a plate. The *ghee* was burned as incense. Afterward, the cook opened his eyes, held the plate, and threw some of the rice and beans at us, an act considered to be good for our family's well-being. Next he put the vermilion and rice on our foreheads and gave some to the drummers who stopped drumming. The senior drummer applied it first to the Hurki, then to the Thali, and finally to his and the Thali players' foreheads. Soon afterwards, they began drumming in Rhythm C as they spoke, requesting the *Dēbi* to insure our well-being. The *Dēbi* responded that we would be feeling better and that we would return to the United States without any problems.

The concluding phase of the shamanistic ritual then began. The drummers played Rhythm D accompanied by a different song text used for the purpose of dismissing the *Dēbi*. At the same time, the cook's dance decreased in pace, until he sat down, and in his sitting position, gently swung his head. Finally, the drumming stopped and the cook returned to his normal state. The senior drummer was given the plate from which he took the money that had been offered (Rs. 1.25).

The performance outlined above took approximately one hour. Garhwali was the language used throughout the entire shamanistic ritual; the song texts were in Garhwali, and the drummers and cook spoke in Garhwali to each other. However, the rhythms, texts, and dialogues are not fixed; if the *Dēbi* had come from a different region, or if she had been displeased, a different set of rhythms and texts might have been used.

Dancing and Drumming

There are three kinds of dancers associated with Garhwali drumming: those who dance to entertain, the possessed dancer, and the female dancer of the Dholki-Ghungru team. The entertainers are always male, though age and caste may vary. The possessed person may be of either sex, and of any age and caste. The female dancer with the Dholki drummer is always one of his female relatives — wife, mother, sister, etc. A dance for entertainment can be held with the Dhol-Damau, Daunr-Thali, or the Hurki-Thali. Note that, except for the female dancer with the Dholki, the drummers themselves do not dance.

In the Dhol-Damau dances the drummers stand to one side of the dancing area. Usually there is a bonfire not far from the drummer. The bonfire is especially necessary during winters or evenings, and at night. The dancers dance clockwise and counter-clockwise in circular motions in front of the Dhol-Damau drummers. If there is a bonfire, it is in the center, and the dancers dance around it in a circular movement.

The dance performances generally vary in length from two to six hours. It is more convenient to hold the longer dances at night. One of these, the *páṇḍau* (Sanskrit *Pāṇḍava*) dance may start at 9 P.M. and end at 5 A.M. the next morning. During this dance, which is primarily for entertainment, a point arrives at which a person from the dancing party or the (watching) audience becomes possessed by the spirit who the drummers were invoking through their drumming and singing. The possessed person has the same symptoms as we described above in the case of our cook. That is, the possessed person shakes, wheezes, and throws his arms in the air while screaming with full force. At this point, the male dancers (who are not possessed) stand to one side so that the dancing area is left free for the possessed person. The drummers play in a very fast tempo while they sing or talk to the possessed person. The possessed person dances in a circular or semi-circular motion at a fast pace, matching the tempo of the drumming. Then the possessed person stops the drumming by putting his hands over the shoulders of the Dhol player or over the Dhol. He (the 'spirit' possessing the person) chants, sings, or talks to the drummers and tells them his wishes. The drummers test him, and if he is found to be a true spirit, they play the desired drumming with the appropriate song texts until the spirit leaves the possessed person.

In a Dhol-Damau dance a man may be possessed by a hero's spirit, such as one of the five *pāṇḍava* brothers of the *Mahābhārata*. Suppose, for example, that the possessing spirit is the spirit of *Bhīm* (Sanskrit *Bhīma*), physically the strongest of the five brothers. In order to prove that he is possessed by *Bhīm*, the Dhol drummer may test him by asking him to lift a huge log which normally could only be lifted by several men. The possessed man does so. Alternately, the possessed man may end the test by lifting the Dhol player (with the Dhol) on his shoulders and then dancing in the center, either by himself, or with the dancing party. The Dhol player continues to drum and sing as he is being carried by the possessed man. When the possessed man dances by himself, the Damau player remains in his position to one side of the dancing area, and drums and sings from that position. When the possessed man dances with others in a circular motion (carrying the Dhol player on his shoulders), the Damau player follows the Dhol player (and the possessed man) and accompanies his singing and drumming.

The Daunr-Thali players sit on the ground. Those dancing to entertain, dance in the same manner as in the Dhol-Damau dances described above. The Daunr-Thali performances, however, are less often involved in secular entertainment than are the Dhol-Damau dances. Their performances deal more often with spirits and individuals directly affected by these spirits. The typical dance is like that of our cook, which was described above in the section on the Hurki-Thali.

When a person becomes possessed by a spirit, the Daunr-Thali players are brought in to act as exorcists. If the spirit is displeased or is an evil ghost, the possessed person shakes and shouts abuses at the players and the family members who invited the players. The players may either retaliate in kind with even more fierce abuses, or may gently try to persuade the evil spirit to leave his victim. The drummers have varied rituals, threats, and persuasions by means of which they exorcise the spirit. The exorcism may continue for several days before the drummers succeed in driving away the spirit.

The dances of the Daunr and Hurki are similar to those above. The *pawaṛa* 'ballad' dances with the Hurki are for entertainment. The Hurki-Thali dancers generally sit on the ground, although the Hurki player may infrequently stand to play when he is not being accompanied by the Thali player.

The Dholki player usually stands when his female partner is dancing. Both the partners, however, may sit while drumming and singing. The female dancer dances in circular and semi-circular motions, clockwise and counter-clockwise. She uses her feet to mark the rhythmic units with the Ghungrus 'anklets, anklebells'. She also employs movements of her hands, waist, neck and face in her dance performance, but her physical gestures are not as complex as those of the classical dances of India.

The Learning of Drumming

The student learns drumming from the teacher through the method of oral transmission. Although the Dhol-Damau drummers say that all the rules of their drumming are given in a book called *ḍhōl sāgar* 'Dhol Ocean', it is highly unlikely that the mostly illiterate Dhol-

Damau players would be able to understand this book even if it were read to them. The book is written in a highly esoteric style and linguistically is a hybrid of several languages.

A person learns drumming from a teacher by audio-visual or aural-lingual impressionistic techniques. That is, the student watches the teacher's movements and articulation of the strokes on the instrument. The student then practices the stroke or stroke patterns until the teacher receives a satisfactory 'feel' or 'impression' from the student's efforts. These techniques apply for singing also. The student sings after the teacher impressionistically rather than being taught rules of singing. In short, the learning of music in this folk culture follows the same natural principles of learning which underlie the acquisition of child language.

The drummers I employed in my field work had learned drumming and dancing from their family members as well as from some other specialists of their area. Now, however, few drummers are interested in teaching their art to their family members. The number of drummers is decreasing drastically and by the end of this century this rich folk tradition will die. My father and I already found it very difficult to locate drummers. None of the drummers we employed had taught or were interested in teaching their children their traditional profession.

The reasons for this decline are very clear. First, the society is changing very rapidly and as a result the profession is no longer at all lucrative. For example, the Garhwalis of Dehradun and Mussoorie now rarely employ Dhol-Damau in their marriages. I witnessed several Garhwali marriages in the course of my field work, and all of them used modern band music consisting of Western drums, clarinets, bagpipes, etc. The melodies these bands play are taken from the popular music of the Bombay Hindi-Urdu movies. Some boys usually dance in front of the band players in a style which is neither Indian nor Western, but is the typical hybrid style of the Hindi-Urdu movies produced in Bombay. The entire band is dressed in Western outfits such as we see in an English band. Dholki-Ghungru entertainment used to be common in marriages only a few years ago, but this feature was missing from all the marriages I witnessed.

The live entertainment of these folk artists is being replaced by a boom in radio and movie music brought about through transistor radios, phonograph records, tape recorders and movie theaters. The radio stations in Delhi and the major cities of Uttar Pradesh, such as Lucknow, Allahabad, etc., have some regular programs on Garhwali folk music, but they are very few in number. Very rarely, the real folk artists are invited to perform in these programs. Three of my artists (a Hurki-Daunr player and a Dholki player with his wife as a dancer-singer) had once been invited to perform in such a program. Some educated Garhwali singers have tried to imitate the music of these professional folk artists, but such emulations are far from the reality. (Some highly educated Garhwalis have told me that they refuse to listen to these Garhwali programs on the radio because they do not represent the true folk art.) I listened to some of these programs, and found that some of the musicians were singing Garhwali songs modeled after the popular Hindi-Urdu film music of Bombay. Most of the songs were accompanied by such musical instruments as the tabla, sarangi, harmonium and Dholak (of the plains). None of these instruments are Garhwali folk instruments. Unfortunately, the real folk artist is neither literate nor educated enough to fight for his rightful place on these radio programs.

I should note that some Garhwalis think that a radio station in this region may help the Garhwali folk artist. In 1974-75 the Chief Minister of Uttar Pradesh was Mr. H.N.Bahuguna who is a Garhwali. Garhwal University has been built through his efforts and the people of Garhwal, through the leadership of Mr. Bahuguna, are expecting more developments in this region, including radio and television stations.

The rapid spread of modern education has rationalized the average person's behavior to such an extent that fewer people now resort to exorcism or other shamanistic rituals. In a village twenty-five years ago a sick person's family would have sought the aid of a priest, shaman, folk medicine man, or an Ayurvedic doctor (one who practises the indigenous system of medicine). Today, doctors, hospitals, clinics, and dispensaries equipped with modern drugs have reduced the need for the services of the priest, shaman and Ayurvedic doctors.

Other traditional roles of these folk drummers are also no longer in demand. The products made by the drummers cannot compete with machine-made goods. The combs made by the *baddi* and clothes sewn by the *auji* (Dhol-Damau) drummers are being replaced by factory made combs and fashionable clothes tailored and sold in shops.

Social pressures, as well as the reduced demand for their services, are contributing to the decline of drumming. Those drummers whose children or other relatives have received a modern education say that their children try to discourage their drumming and try, directly or indirectly, to persuade them to leave their traditional professions. This is because drummers are usually from the *silpkār* castes who were considered untouchables by the *rajpūt* and brahmin castes, and drumming is a reminder of their low-caste status. The educated *silpkār* men are trying their best to make their fellow caste members feel that they should take advantage of their new rights and privileges. The Constitution of India calls the *silpkār* castes a 'scheduled class'. The governments at all levels maintain special preferences and job quotas for these castes. Their children have access to free educational facilities. The newly educated *silpkār* does not want to identify himself with his traditional roles since the traditional roles betray his so-called 'low-caste'. The radical modernization of the Garhwali society and culture is most conspicuous in the scheduled castes. (Anthropologically, the entire nation is experiencing modernization. See Singer 1972 for a more detailed study of the modernization of Indian traditions, and for Indian untouchability in general, see Mahar 1972.)

The Mahābhārata Folklore

The Garhwali area has a very rich folklore and is especially rich in folk literature, most of which centers around mythical characters such as gods, goddesses, demi-gods, demons, ghosts, and fairies. There is also an extensive folk literature concerning human heroes — kings, queens, brave warriors, lovers, etc. The lore of even one of these characters — for instance, of the god *Nirankār* 'formless god' — would be sufficient to fill a book.

The most extensive body of folklore is that based on the *Mahābhārata* tales. The classical *Mahābhārata*, written in Sanskrit, is the longest epic in the world, comprised of over one hundred thousand couplets. It is probable that the classical epic was based on pre-Buddhistic (ca. 500 B.C.) tales present in the folklore traditions of the Aryan tribes. The present-day Garhwali *Mahābhārata* stories retain the basic frame of the classical epic. Innovative details, however, give it a personality of its own.

The development of the *Mahābhārata* tradition from its earliest form to the Garhwali form of today seems to have this pattern:

Folk	→	Classic	→	Folk
(pre-Buddhistic stories)		(Sanskrit epic)		(Garhwali stories)

The Sanskrit epic and the Garhwali *Mahābhārata* stories share the following basic outline.

The *Mahābhārata* relates the struggle for sovereignty of two segments of the royal Kuru family — the Kauravas and Pāṇḍavas. The Kurus were Kṣatriyas (warrior or royal class) from an ancient

Aryan tribe of Northern India. Their capital was at Hastināpura, near present-day Delhi. There were two brothers, the eldest of whom, Dhṛtarāṣtra, was blind. As a blind king cannot rule, his younger brother Pāṇḍu ruled in his stead.

Gāndhārī, the wife of the blind de jure king, gave birth to one hundred sons in one delivery. These one hundred sons were known as the Kauravas. The eldest of them was Duryodhana.

The de facto king, Pāṇḍu, had two wives — Kuntī and Mādrī. Kuntī gave birth to Yudhiṣṭhira, Bhīma, and Arjuna. Mādrī gave birth to Nakula and Sahadeva. Pāṇḍu's five sons were called the Pāṇḍavas. The eldest of them was Yudhiṣṭhira.

After the death of the de facto king Pāṇḍu, as all the Kauravas were both evil and stupid, while all the Pāṇḍavas were both good and intelligent, Dhṛtarāṣtra made Yudhiṣṭhira, the eldest son of his brother, the heir-apparent. Dhṛtarāṣtra's own sons, the Kauravas, felt they had been cheated, and were jealous of the Pāṇḍavas.

Draupadī, the wife in common of the five Pāṇḍavas, was the focus of much of the conflict between the cousins. Another important character in the story was Kṛṣṇa (or Krishna) who fought on the side of the Pāṇḍavas because they were righteous.

After several battles for the Kuru kingdom, during the course of which all the evil Kauravas were killed, the righteous Pāṇḍavas emerged triumphant. (See Rajagopalachari 1950 for an English translation of the *Mahābhārata* stories.)

The above is the skeleton of the story. The classical epic and the Garhwali tales each contain episodes not found in the other. For example, the story of the encounter of Hīt, the mythical relative and disciple of the god Nirañkār, is unrelated to any episode in the Sanskrit epic. The worship of Hīt and Nirañkār is the duty of the untouchable *silpkār* caste. During this worship, untouchability is ignored, and Brahmins and Rajputs participate in joint worship at the home of a *silpkār*. The Sanskrit *Mahābhārata* contains no indication of characters or customs related to the worship of Hīt and Nirañkār.

Similarly, the Garhwali tales lack any reference to the epical story of an encounter between the Pāṇḍavas and a Yakṣa (demon) at a forest pond. This is surprising, as the Yakṣas are alleged to live in the Himalayas. (See, for example, the *Meghadūta* of Kālidāsa for an account of the Yakṣas of this area.)

A Garhwali story derived from the classical epic often differs from the epic version in its details. The story of the marriage of Draupadī, for instance, which has a common frame in both versions, differs in the conditions to be met by the man who wishes to marry the princess. The condition in the Sanskrit version is that he must shoot an arrow into a fish hanging at the top of a pole while looking at its reflection in a pool of water below. In the Garhwali version, the suitor must throw heavy lemons into the air and catch them on the ends of his moustache. Only Arjuna's moustache was strong enough to perform this feat, and so he was the one to win Draupadī. (It is difficult to say why lemons were chosen as a test of prowess, but in the Garhwali region, which has over a dozen varieties of lemons and other citrus fruits, there is a lemon called *bijora* which is the size of a large pumpkin.)

Garhwali tales also often include several versions of the same story. The variations between them may be due to dialectological differences. Garhwali includes several dialects: e.g. *ṭiryaḷi* of Tehri, *raṭhwaḷi* of the *Rāṭh* area, *salaṇi* of the *Salāṇ* area, *sirnagariya* of the Shrinagar area, and many more. (Some, but not all, of the dialects are included in Grierson 1916.)

The following ceremony gives an indication of the massive amount of material included in the *Mahābhārata* lore. The ceremony, called *Nauratu mādāṇ* 'the nine night dance', goes from after dinner until dawn, and continues for nine nights. Each night the Dhol-Damau drummers tell a part of the story to the accompaniment of drumming and a dance called *páṇḍãu* 'Pāṇḍava'. Because such a large amount of material was available in the *Mahābhārata* folklore, we decided to concentrate our fieldwork on this area, and specifically, on the Dhol-Damau drumming in the context of the *Mahābhārata* stories.

In addition to being readily accessible, the Dhol-Damau drumming has rhythmic patterns more complex than those of other Garhwali drums, and the cultural content of Dhol-Damau drumming is greater than that of all other Garhwali drums combined. The above features make it an especially suitable subject for study.

Other drums and texts were studied only secondarily. One such text is the Garhwali version of the *Bhāgavata Purāṇa*, a Sanskrit mythological work linked to the *Mahābhārata* by the character Kṛṣṇa, who appears in both. The *Bhāgavata Purāṇa* stories are also featured in the nine night dance as part of the *Mahābhārata* stories.

It should be noted here that the philosophical portions of both the Sanskrit *Mahābhārata* epic, and of the *Bhāgavata Purāṇa*, are missing from the Garhwali stories. For example, the *Bhagavad Gītā* section of the *Mahābhārata*, which deals with abstract, high philosophy perhaps difficult for the folk mind to absorb, is not found in the Garhwali folklore.

The religious use of the *Bhagavad Gītā* and of other philosophical portions of the *Mahābhārata* and the *Bhāgavata Purāṇa* is assigned to the Brahmin priest. The use of the Garhwali versions of these two traditions is assigned to the *silpkār* drummers. The linguistic and ethnic distributional patterns are parallel — the Brahmin priest taking the Sanskrit form and the *auji* drummers the Garhwali form.

In the following chapters the drumming and texts will be studied from a linguistic standpoint, with most attention being given to the Dhol-Damau drumming. The most extensive portion of each chapter is devoted to the Dhol-Damau, and sections describing other drums will use the Dhol-Damau section as a point of reference.

Field Methodology

It is obvious that in the initial stages, the field methodology of a native scholar will differ from that of the non-native. The native scholar, born and raised in the culture under study, will be already familiar with the language and with most aspects of the culture. He can therefore begin immediately to study the culture (in this case, the music of the culture) from the point of view of his academic discipline.

I was born and raised in a village near Pauri which used to be the headquarters of the Pauri and Chamoli tehsils (counties) of the Garhwali region. I speak Garhwali and Hindi-Urdu as my mother tongues, so I had no difficulty with either the language or the culture. My knowledge of the culture enabled me to organize the fieldwork more efficiently in terms of both time and money.

My field work was also facilitated by my prior experience in linguistic work on Garhwali (Chandola 1956, 1962, 1963, 1966) and in musicolinguistics (Chandola 1969, 1970, 1973, 1975).

Although our (mine, my wife and son's) first choice of location was Mussoorie, we found Dehradun preferable for several reasons. While both are in the Garhwali speaking region, the cold in Musoorie from October to March is prohibitive, and would have discouraged both folk artists and classical musicians from living there. The majority of the population of Dehradun is Garhwali. The city has an academic atmosphere, and is a center which serves as a meeting place for the best talents of the Garhwali region. It was easy to contact Garhwali musicians here trained in classical music, and we found their services as consultants very useful.

Our first step was to rent a residence large enough to include space for office work and for the housing of our folk artists. I then established contacts with the artists around the area of Pauri. I used my father as a sort of free agent to locate the most competent teams of folk artists and persuade them to live with us in Dehradun. One frustration we encountered in this effort was that some teams refused to come as soon as they found that their music would be recorded; they superstitiously feared the loss of their voice once it was switched to a recording machine. Most teams, however, were very cooperative and were eager to be recorded.

When we had located a team of folk artists and established them in residence, we gave them a few days time to feel at home, and to remove the social barriers between us and establish mutual trust. Then we fixed a schedule of times for recording and for analysis. (This schedule was at times dependent upon the vagaries of the electricity supply.)

In addition to folk artists, I hired classical musicians part-time. These were two percussionists to analyze the drumming and two notation writers to prepare the song texts. The percussionists taught tabla, dholak, *nāl* and pakhawaj in schools and colleges in Dehradun. All but one of the classical musicians were college-educated and had professional degrees in music. One was college-educated with traditional training in classical music, and was associated with All India Radio at New Dehli as an expert on Garhwali folk music.

The classical musicians were not usually present during the recording sessions. The percussionists attended the early sessions in order to develop a feel for the folk drumming, and were present in all analytical sessions. The notation writers were only infrequently present in recording sessions, as they worked from the recorded tapes.

Our main goal was to study the drum strokes and their distributional patterns with regard to drumming alone. Our secondary aim was to study the interaction of the tonal and linguistic entities associated with the drumming. With these goals in mind we would hold recording sessions for several days with each team until we had sufficient data to hold analytical sessions. Our procedure in the recording sessions was to ask the folk drummers to play just as they would in a natural context, as though no recording devices were present. There was usually a small audience of Garhwalis present, which added a natural cultural flavor to the sessions. We began by asking the first three teams to give us sample demonstrations of all the rhythms they knew. We followed this with several days of recording the drumming in terms of its actual cultural functions.

Although in some contexts there were no song texts, most sessions were recorded with song texts. We tried in each case to record all possible variants of each song text. There were texts with the same subject but with different titles, and there were variations within one text when it was repeated. For example, the song text entitled *kresn janam* 'Krishna's birth', may also be called *bhagbānai utpati* 'Lord's birth', or just *bhagbānau gīt* 'Lord's song'. In some cases we asked the folk artists to repeat a certain song, as, for instance, the story of *ábimanyu* 'Abhimanyu'. We recorded the same story twice or thrice in order to find out whether the musical form and the linguistic contents were the same each time. We also asked them whether they could sing the same story without drumming. Normally, they very rarely sing without drumming, so in most cases this situation was unnatural for them. However, they found it natural when we asked them to narrate the same story in normal language (prosaic form) which means without singing, drumming, or dancing. Thus some texts were recorded several times in three ways — song text with drumming, song text without drumming, and texts without any music. In doing this multiple recording of one story I sometimes left a gap of several days between recordings. The results were very revealing, and will be discussed in the section on textual aspects. This is why the Appendix contains more than one musicolinguistic version of one story. The normal language version of each song text is based on the normal (non-musicolinguistic) pronunciation of the folk artists of that particular text.

The folk artist's view of historical, geographical, and other aspects of a text differs from the scholarly interpretation. After the recording session I would ask the artists for their interpretation of the text. An example of the discrepancy between the folk view and the view accepted by scholars is folk etymology — a linguistic phenomenon. Two folk artists told me independently that the word *podnya* or *potnya* 'mint' is derived from *putna*. The word *putna* is from the Sanskrit *Pūtanā*, which is the name of a demoness. She was ordered by her master Kaṁsa to kill the baby Krishna by nursing him with poisoned milk, and was killed in the process. The folk artists say that a plant grew on the spot where the demoness fell down. This plant, which is mint, was therefore, called *putnya*, meaning 'born of *putna*'. The demoness died while exhaling long breaths which produced the aromatic smell in mint. The above is the folk etymological explanation. The actual linguistic etymology of *putnya* or *pudnya* is from the Persian word *pudīnā* 'mint'.

Another instance in which the folk interpretation differs from the scholarly is their view of the school attended by the young boy Abhimanyu in the *Mahābhārata*. The folk artist thinks that the school of Abhimanya was just like the schools found in the Garhwali area today, although today's school system was founded by the British. The actual word *iskūl* 'school' occurs in one Abhimanyu story, rather than a Sanskritic synonym.

There are various phonological means by which a performance is made esoteric. As was seen above, folk etymology is a source for an esoteric meaning of a word. A phonological device for adding an esoteric touch to a performance where spirit invocation is involved is to use words like *hō*, *hūṭ*, and *hōṭ*. These words are an indication that the spirit has come. There are several other linguistic ways to suggest the esoteric nature of the performance. Besides linguistics, music is also one of the main devices to convert normal language into an esoteric language, and I have kept records of how the folk artists make a performance an esoteric phenomenon by the use of musicolinguistic devices. (Esoterics, of course, must be considered a separate multi-disciplinary field in its own right).

After we had sufficient data from the recording sessions, we started the analytic sessions. With the first three teams we began with the tape which had the sample demonstrations of all the rhythms they were familiar with. Then we selected a few rhythms from contextual performances. With later teams, which did not have sample rhythms, but were all actual contextual performances, we separated out all the rhythms from the tapes.

We used the following procedure to analyze the rhythms and their strokes. The two percussionists asked the folk drummers to match the rhythm which they heard on the tape. Then the lead drummer was asked to play his section of that rhythm alone. The subordinate drummer did the same, and then both artists played together, matching the rhythm on the tape. This procedure was repeated as many times as necessary, according to the complexity of the rhythm.

The folk artists were asked to play at the slowest possible speed so that the quality and quantity of the strokes in a given rhythm could be observed clearly. In some cases the drummers were not able to reduce the speed or tempo of a rhythm to the extent the analysts wished. This was because some rhythms, according to the drummers, are always played at a high speed. In other words, the drummers impressionistically learned to play some rhythms always with a slow tempo, some with a fast, and some with a medium tempo.

The longer rhythms were the most difficult to analyze. We asked the drummers to count the occurrence of separate strokes and found, to our surprise, that they didn't know what numbers of various strokes were involved in a rhythm. Even more surprising was that they played exactly the correct quantity and quality of strokes. Thus, it was established that the folk artist, to a great extent, learns his music impressionistically, the way a child learns his first language.

We also asked the drummers to teach us all the strokes and a few simple rhythms. The drummer, now acting as a teacher, would sit or stand behind the learner. The drum was in front of the learner. To teach the strokes which were 'stick' or 'slap' strokes, the teacher would hold the learner's hand and strike the drum with it. Where fingers other than in the slap position were involved, the teacher would demonstrate the finger position of a particular stroke over the drum face. In this way we learned the articulatory mechanism of each stroke.

We photographed every stroke position with the help of a professional photographer and recorded each stroke separately. During the analytical sessions we devised several techniques to describe a stroke. Here we faced certain interesting aspects of educational anthropology. As a linguist, I wanted to describe musical sounds and their patterns in the manner of linguistic sounds. The two percussionists, on the other hand, viewed this music as they view their classical music. In South Asian classical music all drum sounds have been given impressionistic names. Consider the tabla (a pair of drums). The open (loose) sound produced by the index finger on the face of its right hand drum's corner is called *nā*; the open sound produced by the same finger in the middle of the drum face is called *tin*; the flat (tight) sound made by the same finger in the middle is called *ti* or *ṭa*, and so on. The open sound in the far corner of the left drum's face is called *ge* or *gin*, etc. The sound *nā* of the right drum and *ge* of the left drum can be produced simultaneously, and the total impression is called *dhā*. The entire tabla pedagogy is based on this naming principle. My classical percussionists felt compelled to give names to every distinctive sound of a folk drum in our field work. In the beginning I suggested that they name a drum sound algebraically or alphabetically (as I have done in the following chapters). They could do it, but they found it time consuming as they would have to think first according to the pattern of naming a drum sound impressionistically, and then convert it for me into an alphabetic symbol. Then I realized that, essentially, it wouldn't make any difference as long as every distinguishable stroke was named distinctly. So, my classical percussionists named every distinguishable sound (stroke) in the style of classical drumming, and I later changed this to alphabetic symbols of my own.

Neither my method nor that of the percussionists meant anything to the folk drummers, as no level of their learning or teaching includes the methodology of classical drumming. From the standpoint of linguistics, classical drumming as well as folk drumming can be described by the same methodology. (See Chandola 1969 for an application of this methodology to the tabla.)

It was easier to work with the classical musicians who were responsible for writing the notations of the song texts, even though their conventions were also based on the methodology of South Asian classical music. They, for example, designated the tones with the Indic names *sa*, *re*, *ga*, *ma*, *pa*, *dha*, *ni* which I changed to their well-established alphabetic names C, D, E, F, G, A, and B, respectively. (For more on the linguistic study of South Asian classical music, see Chandola 1970, 1973, 1975.)

The field procedures I used can be summarized as follows:

(1) Ask the folk artists, one team at a time, to stay and work with you for as many days as are felt to be necessary.

(2) Record their rhythms and song texts. (Use a good portable tape recorder and strong tapes. My portable tape recorder had a small transformer as well as a battery charger, and could also work with battery cells. The tapes must not only be sensitive, but also strong, as they must be frequently moved back and forth on the tape recorder during analysis.)

(3) Observe the artists' drumming, dancing and singing, while making note of points to discuss later with the drummers and analysts.

(4) Ask the classical percussionists (analysts) to sit with the drummers while the drummers repeatedly play after a rhythm being played on the tape.

(5) With the help of the percussionists analyze all the rhythms one by one in terms of the quality and quantity of their strokes. This analysis is done in the presence of the folk drummers. Discuss any points with the folk artists and analysts.

(6) Ask the drummers to teach both you and the analysts all the strokes.

(7) Photograph and record each drum's stroke positions and sounds separately.

(8) When there are no sessions with the drummers, the song texts on the tapes and the tape recorder are given to the notation writers. Discuss with the notation writers any points which come up at any stage of their work.

(9) Utilize the time when there are no sessions to review notes and past analyses and procedures. Determine whether any changes in procedure are necessary.

It must be noted here that these field procedures will vary with the investigator's background, goals, and local conditions.

II
THE PHONETIC MECHANISM

General Remarks

In this chapter we will describe the structural parts which are directly involved in the articulation of a rhythmic instrument sound. Phoneticians are concerned with three things in connection with the phonetic articulation of a sound: the place of articulation, the articulator, and the manner of articulation.

The drum's main place of articulation is its round face, which is usually made of skin. The place of articulation may also be made of shell or metal, however, as some drums employ one or more areas of the shell or another part of the drum as a place of articulation. In the Dholak played in the adjacent Indo-Gangetic plains, for example, the portion of the shell adjacent to the rim is used as a place of articulation for thumb strokes, in which the drummer wears a metal ring on his thumb with which to strike the rim of the drum.

Although the face of the Thali (plate) is made of metal rather than skin, the Thāli can also be considered as an articulator because it is dropped over the rim of a wooden container (Pathu) which serves not only as a resting device, but also as a sound chamber and a place of articulation. That is, the Thali produces strokes when it has been dropped over the rim of this round hollow wooden container.

In the case of the anklebells which are used in dancing, the feet strike the floor, which then becomes the place of articulation.

Some percussion instruments have a device whose purpose is to vary the pitch of the sound. For example, the Hurki has a loop in the middle of its shell. This loop interlocks with the string which links the two faces of the Hurki, and is also attached to the sling which goes around the shoulder of the player. The player rhythmically pulls the loop up and down by pulling the sling up and down, thus making the drum face loose or tight for a stroke, and consequently making the stroke different in pitch. It should be noted here that the pitch variation of the sounds produced on the Hurki has no correlation with the pitch system employed in the singing of the player.

Although all the instruments described here have indefinite pitch, some general remarks can be made about their pitch patterns. Normally, one face of the drum has a lower pitch than the other. The lead drum always has a pitch lower than the subordinate drum. Thus, the Dhol, Dholki, Daunr and Hurki have lower pitches than their corresponding subordinate instruments — the Damau, Ghungru and Thali. (The Thali is the subordinate instrument for both the Daunr and the Hurki).

The round face of the drums and the Thali can be divided into several parts according to the place of articulation used to produce the sound, e.g. rim, corner, center, etc. Generally, if the sounds are produced by fingering, the instruments in question employ at least two parts — corner and center. The stick and knee strokes may involve only one part, normally the center. The corner is usually the near corner, where near corner means that corner which is nearer to the hand or knee. That is, the upper corner area is the near corner for the hands. A stroke sometimes employs more than two areas, as in the sliding stroke called 'ghuraunu' (*ghurɔṇu*) which starts at the near corner and continues down to the far corner.

The articulators are fingers, sticks, knees, etc. A drum may employ one or more articulators, e.g. the Dhol employs hands (fingers), stick and knees, while the Damau employs only sticks. No drum, however, uses only knees. In the case of anklebells, the bells or the 'belled foot' itself is the articulator.

The manner of articulation involves the manner in which pressure is applied to a stroke. One type of stroke produces a hum which we will call an 'open' sound. When the articulator is pressed against the face in such a way that the sound is flat, we call it a 'closed' sound. The contrast between 'open' and 'closed' can be equated with the contrast of 'voiced' and 'voiceless', e.g. the contrast between the *b* and *p* sounds of English. Some instruments, e.g. the anklebells, do not have this 'open' versus 'closed' contrast.

Diagrammatic representations of the places of articulation and the articulators can be made in various ways. One for drums is suggested below:

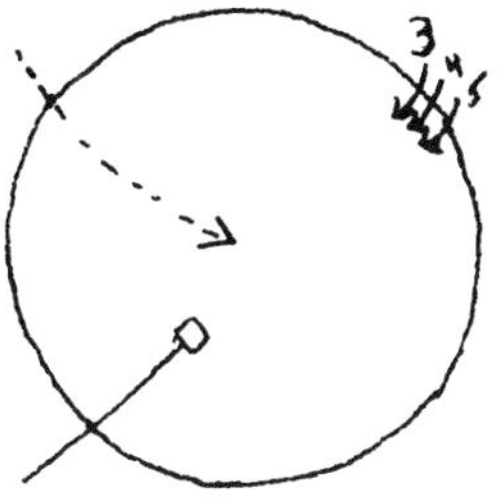

Figure 1

The circle represents the round face of a drum or plate. The stick is represented by a dotted arrowline striking the center of the circle; the fingers (3-5) are represented by the undotted arrows striking the near corner; the hammer represents the knee striking the center. The manner of articulation, e.g. 'open' and 'closed', can be indicated by writing 'o' and 'c' in front of the arrowhead or the square of the hammer. That is- - →c means 'closed stick' stroke, and—▭ o means 'open knee stroke' where stroke means sound.

Now a sketch of the articulatory mechanism of each drum will be given below. We will start with the biggest pair of drums and end with the smallest pair.

The Dhol

The Dhol (*ḍhōl*) and the Damau (*damɔ̃*) make a pair. While the former must always have the latter as an accompaniment, the latter can be played alone in certain contexts. The Dhol is the largest of all Garhwali drums. It acts as a bass drum in relation to the smaller shelled Damau. Here is a general description of one of the Dhols used in our field work.

The Dhol is a bi-lateral (two-faced) barrel-shaped drum. The face on the right side is made of male deerskin and the left of a goatskin. In the absence of a male deerskin, a thick male goatskin is used.

The diameter of each face is 15 inches. The two faces are tied over either end of a copper or brass shell. The length of the shell from one rim to the other is 52 inches. The circumference is 52 inches at the rim and 58 inches at the center.

The skins (or the faces) are linked to each other by means of a cotton string which is woven over the outside of the shell. We will refer to this string as the 'tying string' or 'brace'. The tying string holds the skins which are folded at the rim over a leather ring or hoop (made of goatskin). This ring has 12 holes for each face. The tying string passes through one hole of one ring and goes through the hole of the ring on the other side until all the holes on both sides have been woven together. Two parallel parts of the tying string are interlocked by a cotton loop which can be moved right or left over the shell in order to vary the pitch of the desired face (skin). (There is, however, no concept of a fixed pitch for either face).

The shell has two hooks in the middle. Each hook has a ring to which the cotton sling or strap is attached. This sling goes around the shoulders of the player. The Dhol-Damau player may stand or sit depending on the context. The Dhol rests on the abdomen of the player when he is standing and on the floor when he is sitting.

Each face of the Dhol has two articulatory areas: corner and center. The corner played is always the one which is nearest to the hand or knee.

The right hand articulators are the right hand fingers, knee and stick. The left hand articulators are the left hand fingers. The right hand articulators use the right face and the left hand the left face. Very rarely (only in one context) both hands use the left side while the right knee is being used on the right side. The sides used are reversed if the player is left-handed.

The stick is about 18 inches long. The circumference of the stick is about 2 inches on the top and 1½ inches on the bottom tip. The stick bends near the bottom end, and it is the bent portion which strikes the face. Various kinds of regional woods are used for the stick.

The Damau

The Damau (*damɔ̃*) looks like a small kettledrum (tympani). It is the high pitched instrument of the Dhol-Damau pair.

One of the Damaus had the following features. The shell is made of brass (iron can also be used). The circumference of the shell is 42½ inches at the rim and 13½ inches at the base (we can call the curved back of the shell the bottom or base). In this case, the base of the drum has a small hole — this, however, is not always present. The face is made of deerskin or cowhide which is tied over the rim of the shell. The diameter of the face is 14 inches from the top to the bottom of the rim, and 13 inches from the left to the right side. The shell in this case is not completely round, although they sometimes are. The skin at the rim has 32 holes and is held over the shell by a tying string or brace (made of leather) which is knit over the shell in a criss-cross manner connecting each hole of the skin to a leather hoop or ring around the base. The shell has two leather hooks attached to its upper rim. A cotton sling or strap is attached to these hooks and is worn over the shoulder of the player. The Damau hangs down between the naval and the upper thighs of the player with the face upright.

The Damau face employs only the center area for articulation. There are two sticks, one for each hand, that strike the center area. Each stick is 14 inches long. The circumference of the stick is 1½ inches at the top and about 1¼ inches at the bottom tip. The sticks are slightly curved towards the bottom tip, and the maximally bent portion comes into contact with the skin. The sticks are made of various regional woods.

The Dholki

The Dholki and Ghungru make a team. The Dholki functions as the bass drum in relation to the high pitched Ghungrus. The shape and structure of the Dholki are like that of the Dhol. The word 'Dholki' means 'small Dhol' where the suffix *-ki* is a diminutive attached to the noun stem *ḍhōl* 'Dhol', changing to *ḍhol*.

The barrel-shaped shell of this bilateral drum is made of wood and may vary greatly in size. As the *baddi* drummers have to travel often, they keep a large Dholki in their homes and carry a small one for performances given while they are traveling.

One of the Dholkis used in our field work had the following measurements. The shell's length from one rim to another is 18 inches. The circumference is 31 inches at the rim and 38½ inches at the center. The diameter of each face is 9 inches. The two faces are made of goatskin and are folded at the rim over a leather or bamboo ring (hoop) which has nine holes for each face. The tying string links the two faces together by weaving between the holes of either face in the same manner as for the Dhol. Small cotton loops or iron rings are attached to the tying string as they are in the case of the Dhol. The cotton sling (strap) is tied to the two ends of a strip of the tying string which stretches lengthwise over the shell. As with the Dhol, the player may stand or sit to play, depending on the context.

The Dholki has two articulatory areas in each face: corner and center. It is played with both hands used as articulators. The palm and fingers of both hands produce the strokes. The left hand uses the left skin and the right hand the right skin. Unlike the Dhol, the two hands are never both used on the same side of the Dholki.

The Ghungrus

The word 'Ghungru' (Garhwali *ghuñgru*) means 'ankle bell'. The Ghungrus are small bells attached to two or three strings or leather belts. The belled strings or belts (anklets) are tied to both ankles of the female dancer. The dancer strikes her feet against the ground to shake the bells rhythmically.

The Daunr

The Daunr and the Thali make a team. The Daunr (ḍɔ̃r) shares some features in common with the Dhol. For example, like the Dhol, it uses both a stick and fingers to produce strokes. The Daunr differs from the Dhol, however, in size and shape.

One of the Daunrs is described as follows. The Daunr shell has the shape of an hourglass. It can be made of copper, brass, or, rarely, of wood. Its length from rim to rim is 6½ inches. The neck of the shell (the middle part) has a 15 inch circumference. The circumference of the shell at the rim is 25 inches. The two hollow faces are covered with goatskin tied to each face with a hoop around the rim. The circumference of each face, with the hoop, is 28 inches. The diameter of each face is 8 inches without the hoop. The braces (or the long tying string) cross over the length of the shell passing through the nine holes of each face's hoop. Another string is attached to the braces over the neck (the middle part) of the shell. This string can be moved towards the left or right in order to raise the pitch of the desired side.

The Daunr player sits on the floor and places the Daunr between his knees, or occasionally, under his leg. The right hand uses a stick. This stick is approximately 10 inches long. Its circumference is 1 inch at the top (which is held in the fist) and 1¼ inches at the bottom tip. The bottom tip comes in contact with the drum face in the case of certain closed strokes. The stick bends a little near the bottom, and it is the maximally bent portion which strikes the drum face in the case of open strokes.

The Pathu

The Pathu (singular *pắthu*, plural *pắtha*) is a round wood or metal container used for measuring grain. (It will hold approximately four pounds of grain). Pathus vary in shape and design. The one used in our field work had the following features. The Pathu used for the Thali playing is made of wood. Its circumference is 20½ inches at the top and 22 inches at the bottom. That is, it gradually becomes wider from top to bottom. The thickness of its rim is ½ inch. Its height from bottom to top is 5½ inches. The Thali is placed over its top (i.e. its open end).

The Thali

The Thali (*thāḷi*) is a round metallic plate on which food is served. They vary in size and shape. The one used in our field work was made of bronze, and bronze Thalis are those most used for drumming. The Thali's sides (*ḍĩwāḷ*) gradually slope outward, so that the rim of the open end is slightly larger in circumference than the base. (The sides of Thalis vary in degree of pitch, and may be nearly vertical). The circumference of the rim is 28 inches with a diameter of 8½ inches. The player sits on the floor beside the lead drummer to play the Thali. The Thali can be positioned in two ways. One way is to place it over the Pathu. The second way is to place the corner towards the player (the near corner) over his feet, and the other corner (the far corner) on the ground. In both positions the Thali is upside down, and the projected rim rests over either the Pathu or over the feet of the player. The reverse side of the bottom of the Thali is used as the face of the drum. The Thali placed over the Pathu produces open as well as closed sounds. The Thali placed over the feet produces only open sounds. The former was played with one of our Daunr-Thali teams and the latter with the Hurki-Thali teams.

The Thali Horn and Sticks

The deer horn used as a beater of the Thali varies in size and shape. The one used in our field work was approximately five inches long. It strikes the right corner of the Thali which has been placed over the Pathu.

The more common way to play the Thali is to place its near corner over the feet and use the two wood sticks as beaters or articulators. These also vary in size. The two sticks made of regional wood, which we used in our field work, were nine inches long with a one inch circumference. Each stick bends near the tip. The maximally bent portion of the stick comes into contact with the Thali face. The Garhwali terms for the sticks used with any instrument are *lā̃kuṛ* or *ḍaṇdi*. The horn is called *siṅ̄g*.

The Hurki

The Hurki and the Thali make a team. The Hurki (*huṛki*) is an hourglass shaped instrument like the Daunr, but with a neck (the middle part of the shell) more narrow than that of the Daunr. The narrow neck is necessary as the instrument is held with the left hand clasped around the neck. The shell is of wood.

One of the Hurkis used in our field work had the following features. The shell is 10 inches long from rim to rim. The circumference of the neck, called *muṭ* 'fist' as it is held in the fist, is 8½ inches. The two hollow faces are covered with stretched goat gut. Each face, with its hoop, has a circumference of 20 inches and a diameter of 6 inches. The diameter of the face without the hoop is 6 inches. The hoop is made of bamboo or fig wood. The skin over the hoop has six holes through which cotton braces (the tying string) pass across the length of the shell, as they do in the case of the Daunr. Another cotton string called *hōlaṇ* is attached to the braces around the neck and can be moved towards either face in order to raise the pitch. The Hurki has a cotton sling (strap) which hangs down from the left shoulder of the drummer. One end of the sling is attached to one end of the *hōlaṇ* (the cotton string over the shell neck producing pitch variation) and the other end makes a loop over the shell neck. The drummer inserts his left hand under the braces and grasps the bare shell neck. He then pulls the drum up and down as he plays. This pulling creates pitch variations in the strokes which are being articulated by the right hand on the right face. The left face is not used to articulate strokes. The Hurki is played with the drummer sitting on the floor.

III

THE PHONETIC DESCRIPTION OF THE STROKES

General Remarks

In a phonetic system, each sound is represented by a unique phonetic symbol. Any two sounds of the system differ from each other by at least one phonetic feature or component. For example, the English sounds symbolized as *p* and *b* differ by only one phonetic component — 'voicing'. The former does not have 'voicing' and the latter does. It is customary to refer to the articulatory components of a sound to describe that sound. Thus, *p* is a 'labial stop' which means that the lips stop and then release the out-going air to articulate this sound. The English sound symbolized as *f* contrasts with *p* in two ways: *f* is a 'labiodental' and a 'spirant' sound. However, if we were to articulate the sound *f* with bilabial spirantization it would not make any difference to the hearer. That is, the hearer would perceive the labiodental *f* and the bilabial *f* as identical. This, then, compels us to treat sounds as phonetic impressions rather than as phonetic articulations. In fact, the *f*'s produced by a talking bird like the mynah, or a talking machine, have nothing comparable to the human labiodental articulatory components in their articulation. Even a human ventriloquist does not articulate the *f* sound as we do normally. Yet we still hear the sound *f* whether it has labiodental components or not.

In musical notation, the tones of the octave are represented by these symbols: C, D, E, F, G, A, B. Both humans and various tonal instruments produce these tones, and it would require a tremendously complex notational system if we should attempt to describe these musical tones in terms of the articulatory mechanisms of humans and the various musical instruments. The tonal system becomes much more general and simple when the articulatory components are not considered as defining characteristics of the tones. The phonetic aspect in this case is oriented towards the way we hear the tone rather than towards the production of the tone. We believe that the impression we receive of a sound is the significant criterion in hearing. Thus, C, D, E, etc., are representations of the aural impressions of the octave tones.

However, reference to the articulation of a sound has tremendous pedagogic value. It is important in teaching the phonetic mechanism of any instrument.

We will describe the articulatory components of a stroke (sound) in order to explain the role of the player and the instrument in producing these stroke impressions. We believe, however, that the ultimate functional phonetic units are the stroke (or sound) impressions, not the features or components of those impressions. A sound or stroke means here an ultimate functional phonetic entity which is an aural impression. Thus, an impression P may be articulated in two or more ways (see the Dhol sounds, for an example). Similarly, it does not matter in how many ways a player produces the tone A on a violin as all such events produce the impression of the same tone, which we represent abstractly by the symbol A.

The stroke impressions a drum makes will be represented by various alphabetical symbols. We will use the alphabetical symbols from J to V for the various sounds (strokes) of a rhythmic instrument, just as the symbols A to G are conventionally used for the tones. It must be made clear here that each set of symbols is particular to one instrument. For example, the stroke L of the Dhol is not the same as the L of the Daunr. That is, a single letter of the alphabet represents different phonetic values or impressions when it refers to different rhythmic instruments. It has not been possible to achieve a common abstract symbolic system to represent all the sounds of all the rhythmic instruments, as has been done in the case of the octave tones, which apply for all tonal instruments. The system of beats is the only symbolic system shared in common by all rhythmic instruments. There is no shared system for strokes (sounds). Our primary goal in this chapter, however, is to describe the strokes (sounds) and the distribution of their articulatory components.

All the major strokes of each instrument are illustrated in the photographs included in this book. In addition, the following method has been devised to illustrate diagrammatically the approximate place of articulation of the strokes. The following figure depicts Dhol Stroke L.

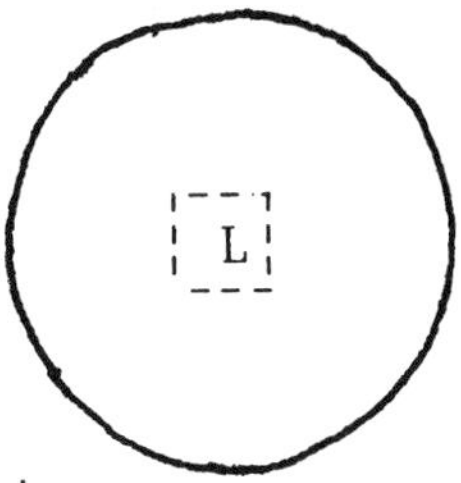

Figure 2 Dhol Stroke L

In this figure, the area where the L stroke is articulated is enclosed by dotted lines. The figure indicates that the stroke is articulated in the center of the drumface (the drum face is represented by the circle).

This diagram can be generalized to apply for more than one stroke, as is shown in the following figure which indicates the place of articulation for the L_1 and T strokes of the Dhol as well as the L stroke.

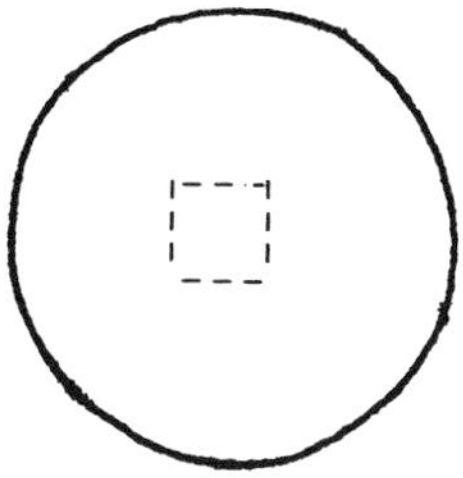

Figure 3 Dhol strokes L, L1 and T

Several places of articulation can be shown in one diagram. The following figure gives all the places of articulation used on the Dhol.

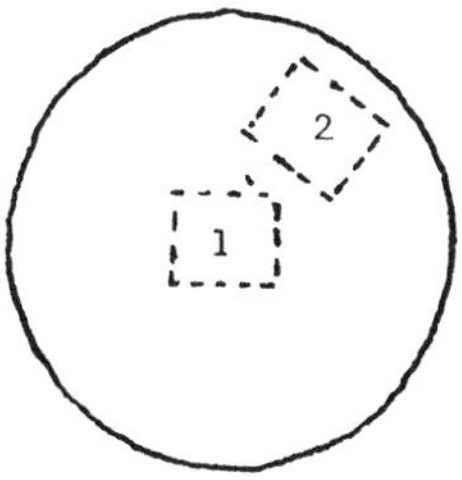

Figure 4 The Dhol Strokes: 1=P, P_1, L, L_1, T, M. 2=N, O

Note that in Figure 4, one circle is being used for both faces of the Dhol, as well as for the strokes articulated by knee, stick, or either hand's fingers. This will be more clear after a detailed description of the Dhol strokes is given later in this chapter.

Figure 4 can be replaced by Figure 5 below:

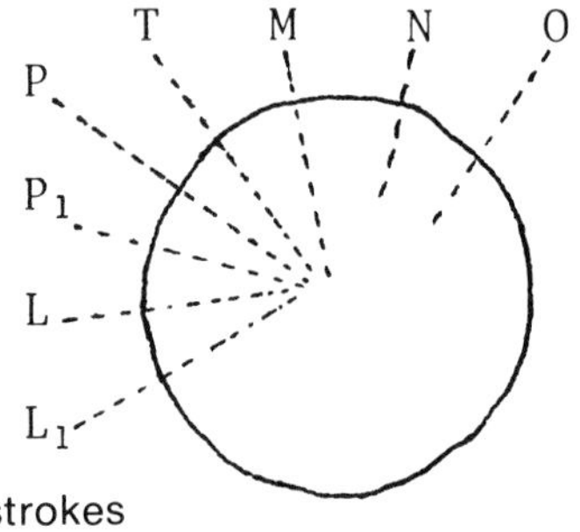

Figure 5 Dhol strokes

The strokes of each instrument, and their articulatory components, have been listed in Tables 1-8. When all the tables given in this chapter are compared with each other a pattern emerges which can be generalized in the following manner. In any given team of the Garhwali instruments, the lead drum has more strokes, and therefore, more articulatory components. The lead instrument is always the larger in the pair. In comparing all the lead instruments, the smaller one has less or equal (but never more) articulatory components than the next larger one. Thus, in the Dhol-Damau team, the Dhol is larger and has more articulatory strokes than does the Damau. Similarly, the Dholki has more strokes and components than the Ghungru, and so on. Among all the lead instruments the Dhol is the largest, and it has more components than the next smaller lead drum, which is the Dholki, and so on.

It should be noted here, however, that these generalizations apply only in Garhwali folk drumming, and not when a larger context of drumming is considered. For example, if classical drums like the tabla are included, these generalizations are no longer applicable. The drums in the tabla pair are smaller than the Dhol or Dholki but have more complexity in their strokes and articulatory components (including rhythms) than does any Garhwali folk instrument — large or small.

Each table below includes a set of abbreviations. These abbreviations are derived from the spelling of the word abbreviated. To abbreviate a term or word we have used its first (one or more) successive and last letters, e.g. Stk is the abbreviation for 'stick', based on the first two letters s and t and the last letter k. This device is both consistent and an aid in easy reconstruction of the full term or word.

The Dhol Sounds

The Dhol is not only the largest Garhwali drum, but also the most complex in every respect from an ethnomusicolinguistic point of view. Not only has it more strokes than any other rhythmic instrument of Garhwali folk music, it also has more articulatory components and combinations. Table 1 shows all the Dhol strokes (sounds) and their respective components. The description of the Dhol sounds given in Table 1 serves as the model for the descriptions of all the successive instruments. The details of the strokes of the other instruments and their articulatory components are easily understood from the tables for these instruments once the complete explanation given for Table 1 has been understood.

	Articulator										Place				Manner		
Stroke	Pam	1	2	3	4	5	Stk	Kne	Let	Rit	Cor	Cer	Let	Rit	Cld	Opn	Sld
N			+	+	+				+		+		+			+	
O	+			+	+	+			+		+		+			+	
S				+					+		+		+		+		
S_1			+						+		+		+		+		
P		+	+						+			+	+		+		
P_1				+	+	+			+			+	+		+		
L							+			+		+		+		+	
L_1										+		+	+			+	
T							+			+		+		+	+		
V		+		+						+	+ →	+		+		+	+
M								+		+		+		+		+	

Table 1 The Dhol Strokes and their components

Table 1 lists the articulatory components involved in producing a stroke on the Dhol. The plus sign '+' indicates the presence of a component for the stroke in question. The symbol '→' means 'starting from + to +', e.g. 'from corner to center' in the case of Stroke V. The fingers are numbered from 1 to 5 where the thumb is finger No. 1. The word 'corner' always means 'near corner' unless otherwise specified.

The abbreviations used are as follows: Pam=palm, Stk=stick, Kne=knee, Rit=right, Let=left, Cor=corner, Cer=center, Cld=closed, Opn=open, Sld=slide.

A complete explanation of Table 1 is given below:

N: The Dhol sound (stroke) represented by this symbol is produced by a left hand slap which uses fingers 2-4. The slap strikes the corner of the left face of the Dhol. The stroke is open.

O: This is produced by a left hand slap which consists of fingers 3-5 plus the palm at the base of these fingers (approximately one fourth of the palm is used). The place of articulation for this stroke is the corner of the left face. The stroke makes an open sound.

S: This is produced by finger 3 of the left hand on the corner of the left side and is a closed sound.

S_1: This is produced by the left hand's finger 2 on the left side corner and is a closed sound. There is no difference in the aural impression of S and S_1. The only difference between the two strokes is that of fingering. The reason the two fingers produce an identical impression seems to be the result of the even functional load of the two fingers. S and S_1 alternate in succession. The strokes are very infrequently heard.

P: This closed sound is produced on the left side center by the left finger 2. Finger 1 moves simultaneously with finger 2.

P_1: This gives the same impression as P but is produced by finger 3. Fingers 4-5 move simultaneously with finger 3. P and P_1 alternate in succession. The case of P and P_1 presents additional evidence that the two units made of fingers 1-2 and 3-5 carry an even functional load. Both units can be symbolized as the stroke P impressionistically.

L: This open stroke is articulated on the center of the right face with a stick held in the right hand.

L_1: This is the same stroke as L except that its place of articulation is the center of the left face. Note that the stick in L_1 is held in the right hand. This stroke alternates in succession with stroke M. It is a very infrequent sound. The strokes L and L_1 give the same impression.

T: The articulatory components of this sound are the same as for L_1 except that T is a closed stroke.

V: To produce this stroke, while the stick is held with the help of other fingers, finger 1 of the right hand is placed over finger 3 of the same hand, and finger 3's tip slides from the corner toward the center, making an open sound. The slide produces a long vibrating hum. This sound is possible only when the preceding left hand stroke is a slap like O or N. That is, V can occur only after N or O has taken place. Thus, the echo of N or O helps the slide of V. Sometimes, in order to get a better slide, the drummer moistens the tip of finger 3 with his saliva.

M: To make this open sound, the drummer, while standing, bends over and tilts the Dhol in such a way that the right face rests on the right knee so that the knee cap can hit it in the center. It alternates with L and, in the case of some drummers, with L_1. This is a very infrequent stroke.

The Damau Sounds

There are only two strokes of the Damau: M and N. Actually, M and N give identical impressions and both can be symbolized by one common symbol, M. The stroke M is produced by the left stick, and N by the right stick, both striking the center of the drum. The strokes are open. The stroke M can be struck very quickly in such a way that the impression given is that of a roll. The components of M and N are presented in Table 2.

	Articulator		Place	Manner
Stroke	Let Stk	Rit Stk	Cer	Opn
M	+		+	+
N		+	+	+

Table 2 The Damau Strokes and their components

The Dholki Sounds

Table 3 gives the articulatory components of the Dholki strokes. There are no new abbreviations in this table with the exception of Lit-Cld for 'light closed'. The stroke sound P is not open like R, nor is it closed like S. The stroke Q is not closed enough to sound like K, nor open enough to sound like J. The T sound, too, is not open like N, nor is it entirely closed. The Dholki is thus the most sensitive drum in this respect. The other abbreviations represent the same interpretation which they have in the context of the Dhol. Thus, for example, the stroke V is marked by the abbreviation 'Sld', which means that it involves a 'slide' in its articulation. The 'slide' on the Dholki is articulated exactly as it is on the face of the Dhol. Note that the stroke symbols of any two rhythmic instruments are not described by the same set of abbreviated symbols. For instance, the N of the Dhol, is not the N of the Dholki, as is made clear by their descriptions in terms of the abbreviated symbols in their individual rows.

The symbols 'Let' and 'Rit' for 'left' and 'right' indicate by the double headed arrow that they stand for 'articulator' as well as for 'place'. That is, 'Let' means 'left hand' in the context of 'articulator' and 'left face' of the drum in the context of 'place'. Similarly 'Rit' means 'right hand' as well as 'right face' of the drum. This means that, contrary to the case of the Dhol, there is no right hand stroke used on the left side of the Dholki, or vice versa.

	Articulator						↔		Place		Manner			
Stroke	Pam	1	2	3	4	5	Let	Rit	Cor	Cer	Cld	Lit-Cld	Opn	Sld
N			+				+		+				+	
M			+	+	+	+	+			+			+	
O			+				+			+			+	
S				+	+	+	+			+	+			
L					+		+		+				+	
T			+				+		+			+		
R				+	+	+	+		+				+	
P				+	+	+	+		+			+		
J			+	+	+	+		+		+			+	
K	+		+	+	+	+		+		+	+			
Q				+	+	+		+		+		+		
V		+		+				+	+ →	+			+	+

Table 3 The Dholki Strokes and their components

The Ghungru Sounds

Like the Damau, the Ghungrus produce two stroke types which are identical in their impressions. These two strokes can be represented by the symbols M and N. M is produced by the bells of the left foot, and N by the bells of the right foot. The bells jingle when the belled foot is struck against the floor. Table 4 represents these two strokes. The abbreviations for Table 4 are: Let Fot=left foot, Rit Fot=right foot, Flr=floor.

	Articulator		Place	Manner
Stroke	Let Fot	Rit Fot	Flr	Opn
M	+		+	+
N		+	+	+

Table 4 The Ghungru Strokes and their components

The Daunr Sounds

Table 5 gives the strokes for the Daunr. The abbreviations in this table are the same as those for the Dhol and the Dholki except for 'Tip', which stands for the 'tip' of the stick as well as for the 'tips' of the fingers. The minus-plus sign '±' means 'optional'. The rare strokes P, P_1, P_2, P_3 give identical impressions but each of them involves different fingers. These strokes always occur in succession from P to P_3. In the case of L the maximally bent portion of the stick strikes the center part of the right face, while in the case of T the tip of the stick strikes the center part of the right face. Very infrequently, L can be repeated in quick succession, resulting in a roll. Like the Dholki, the right hand strokes always occur on the right side of the Daunr and the left hand strokes on the left side. This is indicated by the double-headed arrow over the symbols 'Let' and 'Rit'. This double-headed arrow also indicates that Let and Rit apply to 'articulator' as well as to 'place' (as in the case of Dholki Table 5).

	Articulator							↔		Place		Manner		
Stroke	Tip	1	2	3	4	5	Stk	Let	Rit	Cor	Cer	Cld	Opn	Sld
N			+	+	+			+			+		+	
O			+	+	+	+		+			+		+	
S	±		+	+	+	+		+			+	+		
P			+					+		+		+		
P_1				+				+		+		+		
P_2					+			+		+		+		
P_3						+		+		+		+		
V		±		+				+		+ →	+		+	+
L							+		+		+		+	
T	+						+		+		+	+		

Table 5 The Daunr Strokes and their components

The Thali-Pathu Sounds

In Table 6, which gives the strokes for the Thali-Pathu, the abbreviation 'Thi' is for 'Thali', 'Pau' for 'Pathu' (Garhwali *pấthu*), 'Up' for 'up' and 'Don' for 'down'. The abbreviation 'Stk' is for 'stick', which can be either a stick or a horn. In this case it is a deer horn. The maximally bent part of the horn strikes the Thali to articulate the sounds M and N. In the case of N the Thali is raised and in the case of Q it is dropped, as is explained below. The Thali, which is resting over the Pathu, is first raised up about one inch (on

	Articulator				Place		Manner			
Stroke	Thi	Stk	Let	Rit	Thi-Cor	Pau-Cor	Cld	Opn	Thi-Up	Thi-Don
Q	+		+			+	+			+
M		+		+	+			+		
N		+		+	+			+	+	

Table 6 The Thali-Pathu Strokes and their components

the left corner) by finger No. 3 of the left hand and the (right hand) horn strikes the (right) corner of the Thali in order to produce the sound N. When the Thali is raised up like this (with or without the stroke N) and dropped over the (left corner of the) Pathu, the sound Q is produced. That is, Q is articulated by striking the Thali against the (left) rim of the Pathu. Thus, in the case of Q, the Thali is the articulator and the Pathu corner (rim) is the place of articulation. The action of raising and dropping the Thali is the manner of articulation. The abbreviation 'Thi-Up' stands for raising the Thali and 'Thi-Don' stands for dropping the Thali. In the case of stroke M the Thali remains placed over the Pathu.

The Hurki Sounds

Table 7 gives the strokes for the Hurki. In this table there are only two new abbreviations: Hih and Low standing for 'high' and 'low' pitches respectively. The high pitch is produced by 'pulling out' (explained below) the Hurki with the left hand. The low pitch is the even (or normal) pitch and is produced by not pulling out the Hurki. Note that we have put the pitches 'Hih' and 'Low' in the category of Manner. This has been done because the action of grasping the Hurki by its neck (in the middle) with the left hand and pulling it up and down (out) is considered here as a manner of articulation. Since the left hand has to hold the Hurki by its neck throughout the performance, it can have only right hand strokes produced on its right face, as is indicated by the symbol Rit 'right' in parentheses above the symbols 'Articulator' and 'Place' in Table 7. We also observe here that the closed strokes are always with low pitch whereas the open ones may be with or without (high and low), as is indicated by the sign '±' (minus-plus). Note also that the Hurki is the only lead instrument in Garhwali folk drumming which does not have any stroke with a Sld (slide) component in the Manner column. The slide manner has been present in all the lead drums previously described in this chapter. It seems that the pitch variation present in the Hurki and absent in the other drums is the counterpart of the slide. Thus, it can be said that the Hih and Low symbols in the Hurki Table 7 compensate for the Sld symbol present in the Manner column of the other lead drums.

	(Rit) Articulator			(Rit) Place		Manner			
Stroke	2	3	4	Cor	Cer	Cld	Opn	Hih	Low
L	+			+			+	±	±
S	+	+	+	+		+			+
M	+	+	+	+			+	±	±
T		+	+	+		+			+
K	+			+		+			+
P	+	+	+		+	+			+

Table 7 The Hurki Strokes and their components

The Thali-Stick Sounds

The Thali played with the Hurki uses two sticks as articulators — one for the right hand and one for the left. This Thali is like the Damau in terms of stroke articulation. Thus, only two strokes are articulated on the Thali, and both give identical impressions. Both the strokes are open, and the place of articulation is the center, as is shown in Table 8. The reader should see the Damau Sounds for abbreviations and a discussion of the strokes.

	Articulator		Place	Manner
Stroke	Let stk	Rit Stk	Cer	Opn
M	+		+	+
N		+	+	+

Table 8 The Thali-Stick Strokes and their components

IV
DISTRIBUTIONAL PATTERNS OF SOUNDS

General Remarks

The purpose of this chapter is to show the grouping of strokes. A recurrent sequence of strokes can be called a rhythm or rhythmic cycle. Conventionally, a rhythm is associated with the concept of beats. A beat can be defined as a time space or unit. A rhythm, then, is a set of beats divided into regular spaces of time.

The beat structure, however, is not the point of reference in this chapter. We rather want to demonstrate here how the stroke patterns of two rhythmic instruments are distributed in relation to each other in terms of a rhythmic cycle. We have found that the description of beats is relative to linguistic metrics and to the musical system one (arbitrarily) follows. For instance, the thousands of rhythms that have been developed in South Asian classical music are structured by analogy with the verse sentence structure commonly known as verse meter. An example is the *śikhar tāl* which has seventeen beats. Its seventeen beats and its name suggest that it was developed from the *śikhariṇī* meter of Sanskrit which has seventeen syllables in each line, and in which each line is normally a complete sentence.

Mathematically, however, a rhythm which can be understood in terms of seventeen beats can also be understood in terms of thirty-four beats when played at a faster pace, or eight and a half beats at a slower pace. This is exactly what has happened in South Asian classical music, where the musical text is performed in a rhythm whose beats are evenly distributed, but where beats can be understood in terms of a fraction of a beat. This obviously makes the South Asian system a most complex system of rhythms.

However, this multitude of rhythms employs only a finite set of strokes. It is the stroke system which we can see being improvised in multiple ways to produce thousands of rhythms. We have given the beat structure of a limited number of song texts in order to illustrate their musico-linguistic distribution in terms of conventional time units. In the chapter on textual aspects we have compared the beat structure assigned to the texts by an Indian musicologist with our regrouping of the same beat structure on the basis of stroke patterns. The interaction of two drums, however, can be observed without any reference to their internal beat structure, and this chapter is an attempt in this direction.

The rhythmic cycle is analogous to the sentence. A linguistic utterance is considered complete only when it attains the status of a sentence. Similarly, the completion of a drum stroke performance is done in terms of a cycle.

A sentence is marked by the 'linearity' of linguistic symbols. For example, a sentence like *John is a bright boy* is considered to be a complete sentence. It has symbols which can be understood in terms of concepts (or morphemes) and their sounds, which together make words. We can conceive of a sound sequence in English with a word-initial combination like *br-*, as in the word *bright*, but never a word-initial sequence of *bt-*. This means that English, like any other language, has certain constraints on the linearity of sounds. There are constraints on the linearity of concepts (morphemes) and words as well. We have the conceptual linearity *going* (*go-ing*), but never *ing-go*. We have *John is a bright boy*, but never *Bright a is boy John*. The sentence has another feature besides linearity, the feature of 'selection' or paradigmatic operation, which actually precedes the operation of linearity. (See Chandola 1975 for an elaborate discussion of an evolutionary theory and method of language description.) For example, *John* can be replaced by *Kant*, *Rita*, *he*, *she*, etc. The selection of one symbol affects the selection of another symbol. Thus, if *John* is replaced by *they*, then *is* has to be replaced by *are* or some other plural verb so that we get a sentence like *They are bright*. Thus agreement or concord is an obligatory feature of sentences.

Selection and linearity are the two components which make up the 'grammar' of a sign system. A sign system is a semiotic system. Thus, music, like language, is a semiotic system. The symbols or signs of a cycle are its constituent strokes which develop a cyclic formation based on the principles of selection and linearity. Just as in any other symbolic system, the stroke system has constraints on the operation of its selection and linearity. For example, no rhythmic cycle in Garhwali drumming begins with a closed stroke. The 'slide' stroke V of the Dhol or Dholki can be preceded only by an open stroke. The M sound (stroke) of the Dhol is followed by L. Two strokes can occur simultaneously, e.g. N and O, or N and L of the Dhol, but not S and M, or S and V, and so on. Certain sounds or symbols have relatively more contextual freedom than others, but no sound or symbol is completely context-free.

The linguistic symbols, whether they be sounds or concepts (morphemes), words or sentences, are not referred to in terms of time units in their grammatical descriptions, even though they all possess some kind of rhythmic pattern. Similarly, we have avoided the time reference in describing the rhythmic cycles in this chapter. We have rather described a cycle in terms of its constituent stroke symbols. Since there are two rhythmic instruments involved in most of the drumming, we have also shown the parallel distribution of the two in order to understand how their internal grouping of stroke sequences produces a common harmonious cycle.

The musical material presented in this work could be studied from any one of a variety of linguistic approaches, the choice of approach and the aspects to be emphasized depending on the particular goal the researcher wished to achieve. Recently the notion of 'direction' has been raised by Chafe (1970) and Chandola (1975). To me, the meaning of 'direction' is the 'evolutionary track'. A symbol can be *analyzed* into smaller symbols. Conversely, smaller symbols form or *evolve* a larger symbol. For example, a sentence symbol S can be decomposed into its constituent symbols, e.g. noun (NP) and verb (VP) phrases. This kind of analytical or decompositional approach is exemplified by the transformational-generative models of Harris (1957) and Chomsky (1957, 1965), and the tagmemic models of Pike (1967). On the other hand, in the evolutional formation, meaning followed by sounds makes concepts, concepts make words and words make sentences in a given experience of the speaker (Chandola 1975). The stratificational grammar developed by Lamb (1966) is the only model which emphasizes that a linguistic description can be viewed as coming down from either higher to lower levels or the other way around.

I have assumed here that evolutionarily, a cycle is formed by the composition of strokes or stroke symbols. The cycle itself is a larger symbol where 'larger' means a 'higher level' of compositon. The composition of two or more symbols into a next higher symbol is governed by the principles of 'selection' and 'linearity' (Chandola 1975). We have not explicitly shown here how the selectional and linear rules operate in evolving a cycle, but an evolutionary order of events and operations is implicit in the listing of a cycle.

The Distribution of the Dhol-Damau Strokes

The Dhol, as was seen in the preceding chapter, has a greater range in the quality of sound it produces than does the Damau. The Damau articulates only two strokes, and these can actually be represented by a single symbol impressionistically. Consequently, the Damau tends to repeat more or less identical sequences of strokes within a Dhol-Damau rhythmic cycle, while the Dhol stroke sequences display more diversity in their linear shapes within a given cycle. Below, some Dhol-Damau rhythmic cycles are given in order to illustrate the various distributional patterns of strokes.

Dhol R1.:

⌊N L N⌋ ⌊L N L⌋ ⌊N L L⌋ ⌊O ⌋

Damau R1.:

⌊N M N⌋ . . . .

This notational system represents the rhythmic cycles of each drum of the pair, and the stroke groups within the cycle. Each stroke group may be interpreted as representing one unit of time. The abbreviation R1 means Rhythm 1, e.g. Dhol R1 means Dhol Rhythm No. 1. Similarly Damau R1 means Damau Rhythm No. 1. Each stroke group X is encased as ⌊X⌋ If the stroke group ⌊N L N⌋ of Dhol R1 takes the time unit *y* to be performed, then corresponding to it is the stroke group N M N of Damau R1. If Dhol R1 has four stroke groups consisting of four occurrences of *y*, then the ⌊N M N⌋ group of Damau R1 is repeated four times giving four occurrences of the time unit *y*. In other words, we may say that if *y* is one unit of time, then the Dhol R1 has four such units. The first three stroke groups of Dhol R1 have three strokes each, whereas the last stroke group has only one stroke. Damau R1 has three strokes in one unit. The Damau matches the Dhol cycle by repeating the sequence ⌊N M N⌋ four times. The dots ' . . . ' indicate the repetition of the strokes of the preceding time unit in that sequence. In such a case, the first stroke of a group of the Dhol is matched by the first stroke of the corresponding group of the Damau in a given cycle. Thus, Dhol R1 and Damau R1 can be rewritten as:

Dhol R1.:

⌊N L N⌋ ⌊L N L⌋ ⌊N L L⌋ ⌊O ⌋

Damau R1.:

⌊N M N⌋ ⌊N M N⌋ ⌊N M N⌋ ⌊N M N⌋

Note that our main concern, as was said earlier, is not to deal with the internal timing of the constituent stroke groups of a cycle given by a single instrument. We rather want to observe the interaction of the corresponding individual stroke groups of two rhythmic instruments which together make a harmonious cycle. The encasing of groups indicates that the corresponding stroke groups of the two instruments in a given pair have identical time. We could also present and interpret the rhythms without internally grouping their strokes. That is, there is no need to encase the stroke groups as such. Thus, Dhol R1 can independently be thought of as a stroke sequence N L N L N L N L L O. Similarly, Damau R1 can independently be represented as N M N. Encasing the groups, however, has the advantage of showing the rhythmic and stroke harmony that occurs in the performances of the two rhythmic instruments.

The parallel groups may not have an identical number of strokes: e.g., the last group (group 4) of Dhol R1 has only the one stroke O, whereas the parallel group (group 4) of Damau R1 has three strokes, namely N M N. The time of the O stroke of group 4 of Dhol R1 is the same as that of the N M N stroke of group 4 of Damau R1. The total time of Dhol R1 and Damau R1 must be identical in a given cycle. We thus measure two parallel cycles in terms of their corresponding stroke sequences, which work as units of identical time and space. This does not mean, however, that the internal pauses between two consecutive strokes within a cycle of the same instrument are always even in time. We have ignored pause time in the present chapter for the sake of simplicity.

Dhol R2.:

⌊N L L N L⌋ ⌊N N⌋

Damau R2.:

⌊N N N M N⌋ . . .

Here Dhol R2 has two groups whereas the corresponding Damau R2 has one group. This means that the stroke sequence of Damau R2 has to occur twice in order to match the time of Dhol R2. That is, Damau R2 can be rewritten as:

⌊N N N M N⌋ ⌊N N N M N⌋

Dhol R3.:

⌊N L̃ N N L⌋ . . .

Damau R3.:

⌊N͌ M N͌ M N M N⌋ ⌊N M N N͌ M N͌ M⌋

The superscript '~' means 'roll'. Thus L̃ is rolled L. (A roll is approximately three quick strokes of the stick.) In this R (=rhythm) the Dhol has only one group, while the Damau has two groups. This means that the Dhol stroke group occurs twice in that sequence in order to match the two groups of the Damau in the integrated cycle of Dhol R3 and Damau R3. That is, Dhol R3 can be rewritten as:

⌊N L̃ N N L⌋ ⌊N L̃ N N L⌋

Here we notice that the Damau has more stroke groups than the Dhol. Normally, the Dhol has more stroke groups in a cycle than the Damau. That is, the Damau usually has to repeat the same sequence in order to match a cycle of the Dhol.

It is clear, then, that the total length of a cycle is determined by the drum which has more non-identical groups of sounds. (One could also say that Dhol R3 has two cycles for every one cycle of Damau R3, but we will leave the interpretation of the drum stroke distribution to the discretion of the analyst.) We will now list some of the Dhol-Damau rhythms below, with remarks whenever necessary:

Dhol R4.:

⌊N L L⌋ ⌊N V/O⌋ ⌊N N⌋ ⌊O/T⌋

Damau R4.:

⌊Ñ M N⌋ . . . .

In this Dhol rhythm we see two strokes produced simultaneously. A slant line appears in our notation between any two such strokes: e.g. X/Y (or Y/X) means X of one hand and Y of the other hand strike their corresponding places of articulation simultaneously. Thus, V and O occur simultaneously, and O and T occur simultaneously. (O can sometimes be replaced by N.)

Dhol R5.:

⌊O/T⌒O L M L M⌋

Damau R5.:

⌊Ñ M N M N⌋

In this Dhol rhythm the stroke T and the first stroke O occur simultaneously. The stick (of T) then remains static in that position until the second O is articulated. This is indicated by the superscript slur '⌒' in the sequence O/T⌒O. Notice that the knee stroke M in this Dhol rhythm always rotates with the L stroke.

Dhol R6.:

⌊N/L N⌋ ⌊N L⌋ ⌊N⌋ ⌊S S_1 S S_1⌋ ⌊N/L N⌋ ⌊N L⌋ ⌊O⌋

Damau R6.:

⌊N M⌋ . . . .

The drummers can replace a smaller cycle by a longer cycle within a rhythm. This substitution is done in a ratio of 1:2 with the groups in a given context. The cycle which has fewer strokes or beats is called the *yákharu bā̆ju* 'single-fold rhythm' and the cycle having more strokes or beats is called the *dvā́ru bā̆ju* 'double-fold rhythm'. It should be made clear, however, that in practice the double-fold rhythm is not necessarily two times longer than its corresponding single-fold rhythm. The term 'double-fold rhythm' means simply that it involves more strokes than its corresponding single-fold rhythm. Rhythms No. 7 and No. 8 below exemplify the single-fold and double-fold rhythms, respectively.

Dhol R7.:

⌊N L̃⌋ ⌊N L⌋ ⌊O/T⌋

Damau R7.:

⌊Ñ M N⌋ . . . . . .

Dhol R8.:

⌊N L⌋ ⌊N L⌋ ⌊O/T⌋ ⌊N L⌋ ⌊N L⌋ ⌊O⌋

Damau R8.:

⌊Ñ M N⌋ . . . .

Here we notice that while the Damau cycles of Nos. 7 and 8 remain identical, Dhol R7 has three groups, whereas Dhol R8 has six groups. Thus, the rhythm is determined by the Dhol. That is, Dhol R7 and Dhol R8 are in a 1:2 ratio. This variation of single-fold and double-fold rhythms is one way to break the rhythmic monotony. Another kind of variation is to substitute one stroke for another without changing the rhythmic structure. Sometimes combined strokes may be replaced by non-combined strokes, as is shown below.

Dhol R9. (I):

⌊N L N L⌋ ⌊L O⌋ ⌊O/T⌋ ⌊N/L O⌋

Dhol R9. (II):

⌊N L N L⌋ ⌊L O⌋ ⌊O/T⌋ ⌊N L O⌋

Here the combined strokes N/L in the last group of Dhol R9 (I) are replaced by the N L of Dhol R9 (II), where N and L are not struck simultaneously. The Damau rhythm shared by both is:

Damau R9.:

⌊N M N M⌋ ⌊N M N⌋ ⌊N M N⌋ ⌊N Ñ⌋

Dhol R10.:

⌊N L⌋

Damau R10.:

⌊N M⌋

These two smallest cycles are played when the linguistic texts are very prosaic. The term 'prosaic' refers to the version of the texts which is closest to the normal language (less tonal and less rhythmic). One context in which these rhythms occur is the text called *jācṇi* 'exploratory, inquiry', which is sung when one of the dancers in the dancing party becomes possessed by a spirit. The drummer begins to inquire about the spirit in a version of the language which is less musical. Sometimes the Dhol player keeps his left hand on his ear in this context, and in such a case, the stroke N is replaced by L. That is, the left hand slap stroke is replaced by the right hand stick stroke.

Dhol R11.:

|S S_1| |L L T|

Damau R11.:

|M N M| |N M N|

Dhol R11 and Damau R11 are an example of a light rhythm. The light rhythm is that rhythm which is played with the lowest amplitude. It is played so because a light rhythm is necessary when the drummers are singing, as their singing is audible only when the volume of the drum sounds is low. Thus we have two rhythms which alternate with each other — one which occurs with the song text, and another which occurs without the song text. The drummers may repeat the last lines of the preceding stanza (which is not necessarily metrical) wholly or partially as they play the heavy rhythms. The rhythms from R1 to R10 are examples of heavy rhythms. A heavy rhythm has a high amplitude or volume. The heavy rhythms give the Dhol drummer a chance to think of or remember the next stanza. That is, the alternation of rhythms not only breaks the monotony, but also helps the smooth narration or recitation of the song text theme by providing time for the drummer to remember his next lines.

The Distribution of the Dholki-Ghungru Strokes

One of the rhythmic instruments in a pair, as was noted before, can be played without the other. The Dholki is an instrument which has a high degree of independence because it is not ever necessary for the female singer to dance in accompaniment to it. The Ghungrus articulate only two strokes, both of which give identical aural impressions. Every rhythm of the Dholki can be played without the accompaniment of Ghungru strokes. The first four Dholki rhythms, therefore, will be given below without their associated Ghungru rhythms. The other Dholki rhythms will appear with the Ghungru distribution. Note that the stroke groups of the first four Dholki rhythmic cycles are encased, even though there are no corresponding Ghungru cycles given. This has been done with the assumption that there could potentially be corresponding Ghungru cycles whose stroke groups would then correspond with the encased stroke groups of the first four Dholki rhythmic cycles.

Dholki R1.:

S/K J | N S | N/J | S/K | J N | S/K N/J | ___

Dholki R2.:

M M V | M M V | M V | M P T M/J J

Dholki R3.: (single-fold)

O/J L N | O/J N

Dholki R3.: (double-fold)

O/J L N | O/J N | O L N | O N

Dholki R4.:

O/J N/J J | O/J N/J J | O/J N | N/K N

Dholki R5.:

J N L | K N P T Q P | O/J N P T Q P | O/J N P T Q P

Sometimes L is replaced by N or R in the first group, thus, J N L changes to J N N or J N R.

The Ghungrus may accompany this rhythm with:

N . . . .

The Ghungru stroke N (the sound made by the Ghungrus on the right foot) occurs with the first stroke of each group of Dholki R5. In the next cycle, the dancer uses the M stroke of the Ghungrus:

M . . . .

Thus the N and M strokes of the Ghungrus alternate with each other in the first few cycles. Then two Ghungru strokes occur for each group of Dholki R5 in the following manner:

N M . . . .

This may alternate with the following cycle:

N N | M M | N N | M M

A more complex pattern of the Dholki and Ghungrus emerges in the following rhythmic situations:

Dholki R6.:

(a) O/J N | N/K O N | N/K O N | N/K P T Q P

In the beginning of a stanza the above pattern is played. In the middle of the stanza, a few cycles of the following pattern occur:

(b) N O/J | P T K N | N O/J | P T K N

Before the last line of the stanza, the following pattern occurs for a few cycles:

(c) N O/J O/J . . . .

The last line of the stanza ends with the following cycle:

(d) O S J N | N/J O S | J N N/J | O S J N

The drummer picks up (a) of Dholki R6 immediately after (d). The Garhwali Dholki drummers call parts (b)-(d) *ghirṇi* 'round, circle'. This type of playing resembles the semi-classical singing of Hindustani classical music which is known as *ṭhumrī* in Hindi-Urdu. In classical music, part (a) is called *ṭhekā* 'base'; part (b) is *uṭhān* 'raising'; part (c) is *laggī* 'attachment'; and part (d) is *tihāī* 'third'. Part (d) is called 'third' because the sequence of strokes is repeated three times in such a way that the last stroke of this sequence becomes the first stroke of the next cycle. Thus, in (d) the sequence stroke is O S J N N/J, and the last stroke N/J replaces the first stroke O/J of (a).

It should be noted here that the Garhwali Dholki drummers also play the tabla drums. There is a difference, however, between standard tabla playing and that of the Garhwali Dholki players. The tabla is a pair of drums, one for each hand, in which the right hand drum is called *dā̃yā̃* and the left hand drum is *bā̃yā̃*. The *dā̃yā̃* is played by the right hand and the *bā̃yā̃* by the left. The Garhwali Dholki players, however, play the *dā̃yā̃* with the left hand and the *bā̃yā̃* with the right. This is because the *dā̃yā̃* has more individual finger strokes, whereas the *bā̃yā̃* has more slap type finger positions. In Garhwali Dholki playing, individual finger strokes occur on the left side, and more slaps on the right side. For instance, N, O and T require one finger of the left hand, whereas all the strokes of the right hand require more than one finger. The Garhwali Dholki player, therefore, finds it easier to use his left hand on the right drum of the tabla, and vice versa. (This suggests that the Garhwali Dholki player learns the tabla only as a second instrument.) The tabla and the Dholak (the Dholki of the adjacent plains) are the drums commonly used in the *ṭhumrī* style of North Indian (Hindustani) music. It is difficult to say to what extent the *ṭhumrī* style has influenced the Dholki performance of Garhwali folk music.

The Ghungru rhythms corresponding to (a) and (b) of Dholki R6 have the following stroke patterns:

N . . . .

This means that the dancer may use only the right foot to produce strokes. After a few cycles of Dholki R6 (a-b), she may start the following pattern:

N M . . . .
M N . . . .
N M . . . .

These three sequences occur for sometime, and make the following circles:

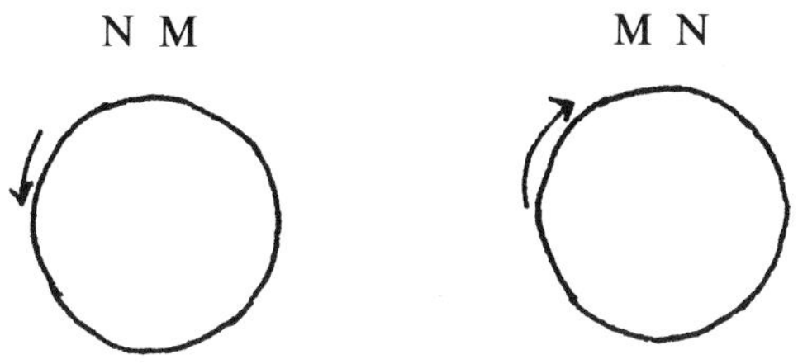

Circle A Circle B

The arrows over the circles indicate that the cycle which begins with the right foot on stroke N makes a counter-clockwise circle, e.g. circle A. The cycle starting with the left foot on stroke M makes a clockwise circle, e.g. circle B. These sequences are the most common patterns in the dance.

The following Ghungru stroke pattern corresponds to (c) and (d) of Dholki R6.

M N N . . . .

The Distribution of the Daunr-Thali Strokes

Below, some Daunr and Thali cycles are given. It should be noted here that the Thali which was played with the Daunr in this case used the horn and the Pathu instead of two sticks (as beaters). Consequently this Thali produces three strokes which are distinct from each other not only articulatorily, but also impressionistically. Thus, the Thali strokes given here are more interesting than those of the other subordinate drums (Damau, Ghungru, etc.) which offer no variety in their stroke impressions.

Daunr R1.:

L S/T O

Thali R1.:

N Q N Q M

Daunr R2.:

T S L/V L

Thali R2.:.

N Q M . . .

Note that the slide stroke V in Daunr R2 is begun simultaneously with the first stroke L, and continues until the second L is struck simultaneously with it. This is indicated by the superscript slur '⌒' in the sequence L/V⌒L.

Daunr R3.:
L N L
Thali R3.:
M Q M
Daunr R4.:
L L   L N L   L L   L/V
Thali R4.:
N Q M   . . .   .
Daunr R5.:
(a) T/S   L   O L   L
(b) P P_1 P_2 P_3 S   O L   O L   L/V
Thali R5.:
M Q   . . .   .

Daunr R5 displays the single-fold and double-fold relationship in (a) and (b) respectively. The identical rhythm in the Thali corresponds to both (a) and (b) of Daunr R5. Note that (b) has more strokes than (a) above, but their cyclic times are identical. It is clear, then, that in Garhwali music, the single-fold and double-fold rhythms do not always have a 1:2 ratio in terms of time. What *is* essential is that the double-fold rhythm must have more strokes than its corresponding single-fold rhythm.

Daunr R6.:
S L/O   L/V⌒L   L/V⌒   L
Thali R6.:
M Q M   . . .   .

Note here how the slide of V in the third group continues as far as stroke L of the last group in Daunr R6.

Daunr R7.:
O L O L L/O L̃ T/S
Thali R7.:
M Q M M Q M M M

The L̃ in Daunr R7 means that there are a few quick occurrences of the stroke L which yields a roll.

Daunr R8.:
(a) L N L   L/V L   T/S   T/S
(b) L N L   L/V L   L   T/S
Thali R8.:
M Q M   . . .   .

The Daunr player continues to change the strokes here and there within the same cycle, as is exemplified by (a) and (b) above. This is done in every rhythm.

The Distribution of the Hurki-Thali Strokes

The Hurki rhythms given below are accompanied by the Thali rhythms which are produced by sticks instead of the horn and Pathu. Playing the Thali with sticks provides a less complex set of strokes than those we observed in the preceding type of Thali, which was played with the Daunr. However, the rhythmic quality and quantity do not seem to be affected by a greater or lesser degree of complexity of stroke articulation in either style of Thali playing. The high pitch (Hih) is indicated by the super diacritic ' ´ ' over a stroke. That is, Ḿ in Hurki R1 below means the stroke M has a high pitch; absence of this diacritic means the stroke has an even or low pitch (Low).

Hurki R1.:

⌊Ḿ M M⌋

Thali R1.:

⌊N M N M N⌋

An example of a double-fold variation of Hurki R1 is given below. The Thali in this case repeats its pattern twice.

⌊T K L Ḿ⌋ ⌊Ḿ Ḿ Ḿ⌋

The Thali, however, can vary independently of the single-fold and double-fold variations of the Hurki cycles. One variation of Thali R1 is as follows:

⌊N M N M N M N⌋

Hurki R2.:

⌊L S⌋ ⌊Ḿ Ḿ⌋

This can be permuted with a slight variation in pitch as:

⌊Ĺ Ḿ⌋ ⌊Ḿ S⌋

Thali R2.:

⌊N N⌋ ⌊N M N⌋

Hurki R3.:

⌊Ḿ⌋

Thali R3.:

⌊N M⌋

These two smallest cycles, which are called *caurās* 'flat' or *phākṛa* 'details', are repeated, and function like the *jācṇi*. (See Dhol R10 and Damau R10.)

Hurki R4.:

⌊M⌋

Thali R4.:

⌊N M⌋

These two small cycles differ from Hurki R3 and Thali R3 in two ways. Hurki R3 has a stroke with high pitch (Ḿ) whereas Hurki R4 has the same kind of stroke without the high pitch (M). The other difference is that Hurki R3 is only played in a spiritual context like that of Dhol R10 and Damau R10, whereas Hurki R4 is played in the context of the ballad songs when there is fast action, such as when the hero (non-spiritual) performs an act of bravery in a battle scene. What is interesting here is that a phonetic difference of one component, namely pitch in Hurki R3 and R4, corresponds to the difference of a spiritual or non-spiritual context.

Hurki R5.:

⌊P⌋ ⌊Ḿ⌋

Thali R5.:

⌊N M⌋ . . .

This Hurki cycle sometimes occurs after the following Hurki cycle (in which case the Thali sequence ⌊N M⌋ is repeated four times).

⌊T K⌋ ⌊L⌋ ⌊Ĺ⌋ ⌊Ĺ⌋

Hurki R6.:

⌊Ĺ Ḿ⌋ ⌊Ḿ Ḿ⌋ ⌊Ĺ P⌋ ⌊P P⌋

Thali R6.:

⌊N M⌋ ⌊N M⌋ ⌊N M⌋ ⌊N N⌋

Hurki R7.:

⌊T K Ĺ⌋ ⌊Ḿ Ḿ⌋ ⌊Ḿ⌋ ⌊S S⌋

Thali R7.:

⌊N M N⌋ . . . .

V
TEXTUAL ASPECTS

Song Texts and the Singers

The texts, as shown in the Appendix, display the following major distributional patterns. A text as a whole is distributed between a lead and a subordinate singer. The subordinate singer is a male drummer (or a male plate player), except in the Dholki performance where the subordinate singer is a female dancer with anklebells. The textual portion of each singer is indicated by arrows. Each portion begins with an arrow and continues until the next arrow or drumming. Drumming is indicated in the song text by the word 'drumming'. An arrow with an upward point (↑) indicates the portion of the unaccompanied lead singer. An arrow with a downward point (↓) indicates the portion of the subordinate singer. An arrow with one point upward and one point downward (↕) indicates the portion common to both singers.

The octave tones C, D♭, D, E♭, E, F, F♯, G, A♭, A, B♭, and B have been written over vowels (or consonants) as is usually done for South Asian music. The space between two occurrences of one or more tones indicates equal time. Two or more tones encased together ideally have the same time unit as a single non-encased tone has. Thus, in a sequence C - F - ⌊GF⌋, there are five spaces: C, -, F, -, and ⌊GF⌋ (the two notes G and F are encased as ⌊GF⌋). These five spaces have equal timing. A notation like 'C-' means 'CC', as 'F--' means 'F F F'. Similarly a vowel like 'ā - - -' means 'ā ā ā ā. The hyphen denotes the prolongation of the preceding vowel or tone. The octave in the middle of the singer's personal register is unmarked. A note from the next higher octave is indicated by a dot over the note. A note from the next lower octave is indicated by a dot under the note. (The singer rarely uses a range of more than the middle octave). A grace note or a slight touch of a tone is indicated by a superscript, e.g., ^{B}A means that the tone A is preceded by a slight touch of B.

Some texts appear with beat numbers indicated on top of the line. It should be made clear here that the distribution of a rhythm into beats is purely an analytic approach of the musicologist, not a technique of the folk artist. The folk drummers have no concept of beats. The drummers and dancers operate in terms of recurring stroke patterns. They play these stroke patterns intuitively or impressionistically, but always accurately in terms of their timing. That is, the timing between individual strokes or the timing between the cycles of a rhythm is always the same. The musicologist, however, cannot distribute a language text over a rhythm without using the concept of beats. Since the drummers do not have any conscious concept of the beats of a rhythm, the analyst must impose his own methodology. This methodology, however, must not distort the data and ideally should grow out of the data. This introduces a crucial point. Musicologists (analysts) differ in background and training. For example, Part I of Dhol text 2 has been analyzed by Anuragi in terms of a 6-beat rhythm. I have changed this to a 12-beat rhythm. Anuragi, an All India Radio folk artist of Garhwali, is a learned musicologist trained in the tradition of Hindustani (North Indian) classical music.

The rhythm type found in Part I of Dhol Text 2 has the following scheme:

Dhol:

N L L N	L N L L	N L O	N T/O
1 2 3	1 2 3	1 2 3	1 2 3

Damau:

N M N	. . .	. . .	. . .
1 2 3			

Here I have put the numbers 1, 2, 3 to indicate the beats for each group of strokes given above. Thus, the rhythm has a meter of a 1, 2, 3; 1, 2, 3; 1, 2, 3; 1, 2, 3 type (comparable with ¾ time in Western music).

In Hindustani music there is a rhythm called *dādrā* consisting of 6 beats with the following pattern:

dhā	dhī	nā	dhā	tū	nā
1	2	3	4	5	6

The *dādrā* rhythm has a meter in ¾ time, or, 1, 2, 3; 1, 2, 3, but it is considered to have 6 beats since its basic cycle recurs after the sequence of six strokes (called *dhā, dhī, nā, dhā, tū, nā* in the tabla drumming system of Hindustani music). Thus, because of the similarity of the Dhol meter to the meter of 1, 2, 3; 1, 2, 3 which is found in the *dādrā* rhythm of the Hindustani system, Anuragi has interpreted the text in terms of 6 beats. I have interpreted it in terms of 12 beats because of the cycle of the Dhol strokes, which recur after a 12 beat rather than a 6 beat cycle. If we follow Anuragi's analysis, the 6 beats cover only the duration of the first two stroke groups of the Dhol cycle—N L L N and L N L L; and the last two groups N L O and N T/O, are covered by another cycle of 6 beats. I preferred to be governed by the above-mentioned Dhol stroke pattern which takes 12 beats time to complete one cycle. That is, the beats shown over a song-text are based on the cyclic length of the Garhwali folk rhythm, rather than on Hindustani classical music rhythms.

The following are the textual situations for the subordinate singer.

(1) Except for the subordinate singer of the Dholki texts, all subordinate singers (who are male drummers) repeat a portion of the text that has first been used by the lead singer in the actual performance. For example, in Part III of Dhol Text 1, the portion *baiṭhi caupaṛa* 'the dice game is set' is repeated until this portion (Part III) is complete musically (in terms of intonation and rhythm) as well as thematically (in terms of the 'dice game'). That is, as long as the subordinate singer continues to repeat these words, the listeners know that the story is now about the dice game. This type of textual repetition by the subordinate drummer can be called a 'literary drone' or a 'textual drone'. It is analogous to the musical drone which is discussed later in this chapter. The textual drone may take forms other than the repetition of the thematic phrase. When the title word or words do not occur in the immediately preceding lines of the lead singer, the subordinate singer may choose a word or words which identify a character in that part of the story. For example, in Part III of Hurki Text 1, the title word is *ḍaũḍya*, which is the name of a god known as *narsiṅ* (Sanskrit *nṛsiṁha*). This part of the story describes the fierce dance of this god. By repeating the word *ḍaũḍya*, the subordinate singer provides a title which means 'this is the god *ḍaũḍya* dancing'.

(2) The second textual situation for the subordinate singer is that he simply repeats wholly or partly every line of the lead singer, as is shown in Part II of Dhol Text 5. In this case he does not make an effort to choose words appropriate for a title.

(3) The third textual situation for the subordinate singer is that he may simply prolong the last vowel of the last word or syllable of the lead singer. For example, in Part I of Dhol Text 5, the subordinate singer simply prolongs the vowel *ē* of the last syllable *lē* of the lead singer. Another instance where this occurs is in the situation preceding loud drumming, as in Part III of Dhol Text 2, where the subordinate singer prolongs the vowel *ā* in accompaniment to the lead singer until the drumming begins. In another case, the singer may not be in a position to improvise his textual part. If he was supposed to sing but has been unable to improvise a part, he may resort to simply prolonging the preceding vowel or syllable.

(4) The last situation for the subordinate singer is that he may not sing at all. This situation may be due to the fact that in prose recitation he is not stylistically allowed to sing.

The most important functions of the subordinate drummer or singer are to help the lead drummer musically and linguistically. Musically, the subordinate singer provides his or her matching rhythmic cycles. Intonationally, the lead singer needs a drone on the basis of which he can maintain an even pitch register. Garhwali folk singers do not use any tonal instruments with these drums, and the subordinate singer performs the function of a drone by repeating a portion of the text, as shown in textual situations (1) and (2) above, or by prolonging the last vowel, as in textual situation (3) above. That is, the intonation of the subordinate singer becomes a reference point in relation to which the lead singer maintains a consistent intonation. Of course it could be said that the lead singer, who is always supposed to be a more mature singer, helps the subordinate singer to maintain a consistent intonation. Indeed, the two singers provide each other with a mutual check for each singer's intonation.

Textually, the subordinate singer provides time to the lead singer not only for a rest, e.g. to take a breath, but also gives him an opportunity to plan the next line. It should be noted here that there is no fixed form of a text. In other words, a story may vary in its details from one version to another. The singers improvise the form of the story every time they sing it, as will be shown later. The lead singer does not have a memorized version of any story which is in the free verse form. Instead, he remembers the broad contents of the story and recalls the specific, narrow details as he is singing. When the subordinate singer is singing, the lead singer is using that time to recall or plan the next musicolinguistic act.

The female dancer-singer in the Dholki texts is an exception to the generalizations made above. Although the Dholki texts clearly demonstrate that the lead singer is usually the one who begins the text and determines the rhythms, the total musicolinguistic load of the subordinate singer in the Dholki text is almost equal to and sometimes even greater than that of the lead singer. There is a sharp textual difference between the role of the female singer and that of the male singer as subordinate singers. The textual content given by the lead singer is complete in itself in the case of the Male-Male situation. For example, in Part II of Daunr Text 2, the subordinate drummer joins the lead singer with the word *sabā*. We know that the story would have been complete in terms of its linguistic contents even without the introduction of the word *sabā* by the subordinate singer, as it is already a part of the text of the lead singer. Again, there is the example from Part II of Hurki Text 1 where the subordinate singer used the word *ḍaũḍya* as a title. The story would still be complete even without this use of the word *ḍaũḍya* by the subordinate singer.

In contrast, the text cannot be considered complete without the addition of the textual portions of the female singer in the Male-Female situation of the Dholki text. For example, in Dholki Text 3 the lead singer begins the next portion of the song with the words *tai rāja ki chayī parbhu jo bhagibāna* 'O Lord, O God, that king had', followed by the words of the subordinate singer *bhagibān jī chayī rāṇi pabana rekhā* . . . 'O God, (the king) had a queen Pavanarekhā (by name) . . . '. The information that the 'king had (something)' is completed by the female singer, who adds that 'it was Pavanarekhā the queen (that the king had)'.

The female singer's dance steps provide very simple stroke patterns compared to the complex stroke system of the Dholki drummer, but the total articulatory load of the female performer is as complex if all her physical movements are taken into consideration. The motions of hand, neck, face, and waist, and the circular motions required in the dance, although very simple in their articulation and arrangement, increase the complexity of her articulatory load. Thus, the female singer of the Dholki texts is not comparable to the subordinate male singers of the non-Dholki texts. The non-Dholki subordinate singers are usually less competent than the corresponding lead singers. This is clear from the fact that the male subordinate learns not only the texts but also the drumming and singing from the lead singer. The listeners or watchers are conscious of the fact that in the Male-Male situation the lead singer carries far more musicolinguistic load, and that much more competence is required on the part of the lead performer. The listeners and watchers do not consider this to be so in the case of the Male-Female situation. Both male and female are considered to be equal load carriers in a given performance.

Textual Variation

The degree of musicolinguistic variation in textual versions of the same story or theme depends largely on the length of the story. The longer the story the more musicolinguistic variation is to be expected, and vice versa. Traditionally, the Dholki texts are the shortest in length. The texts of other drummers are usually longer.

Consider Dholki Texts 3-4. These two Dholki texts are from two different teams of singers, but these teams were both trained by the same teachers. These two texts have the same theme. This theme is known by several names: e.g. *kirsn janam katha* 'the birth story of Krishna', *bhagbānai utpati* 'the incarnation of God', etc. Some components, such as rhythm, remain unchanged. The intonation seems to the average listener to have some changes, but the two intonations are actually very similar. The words are almost the same, except for the musical words (e.g. words without meaning, which are invented to fit the meter, act as a drone, or to produce onomatopoeia) and other idiosyncratic words that mark the style of the individual performers.

When one theme is sung more than once by the same singers, the degree of variation is further reduced. For example, in Dholki Texts 1 and 2 we have two versions (performances) of the same theme sung by the same singers. These two texts have the least amount of variation of all the textual samples we have given here. It can be seen that these singers have some scope for improvisation even in texts as short as these are. For example, the tones for the first occurrence of the word *madusōdhana* are E E E - DC in Dholki Text 1, and F F F E FF in Dholki Text 2.

In Dholki Text 1, the first idiosyncratic stylistic word of the male singer is *bhai*. This is extended as *bhai jo* in Dholki Text 2. The versions of the lead and subordinate singers may also vary slightly. For instance, the lead singer has *nāma ma ca* 'is in the name', while the subordinate singer has *nāma se* 'from the name'. The subordinate singer first joins the lead singer on beat No. 3 of the third cycle in Dholki Text 1, but on beat No. 6 in Dholki Text 2. The subordinate singer begins her singing with the word *madusodhana* in Dholki Text 1. In Dholki Text 2, she drops the first two syllables of the word, and *madusodhana* is sung as *sodhana*. The listener re-edits or reconstructs *sodhana* as *madusodhana* on the basis of its previous occurrences. The partial phonetic deletion of a word on the basis of its immediately preceding occurrences in a similar context is an interesting phenomenom which is very common in Garhwali singing.

In larger texts the scope for improvisation is far greater. However, there are limits or constraints present on every level of performance. Consider the *Abhimanyu* story. The singers were asked to narrate this story singing with and without drums, and with and without singing. (As was noted previously, the singers found it difficult to sing without drumming.) The singers themselves feel that they are giving the same story each time, but on the musicolinguistic level, each version of the story differs from every other version. If you call their attention to the musical differences between several versions of the same story, they will readily tell you that there are several styles (called *bhauṇ*) from which they can choose. A style is marked by a series of intonational patterns. The rhythms also vary from style to style, or from one intonational pattern to another. Normally, the rhythms change when the intonational pattern changes, but it again depends on the choice of the lead singer. For instance, in the Abhimanu story of Daunr Text 2 there is only one rhythm from the beginning to the killing of Abhimanu, while the same story of Daunr Text 1 differs in singing style and rhythms throughout the text. Although the singers think that both texts narrate the story of Abhimanu in the same way, the two versions can be expected to vary in detail. For example, in Daunr Text 1 the assembly of the *Kaurava* brothers takes place first, whereas in Daunr Text 2 the assembly of the *Pāṇḍava* brothers is the first to occur.

An interesting question which arises here is, what do we mean by 'same' and 'different' in terms of musicolinguistic events? One answer could be that what we view as 'different' on one level may be viewed as the 'same' on another level.

Consider the English sound *p* in the words *pin* and *spin*. The sound *p* in each of these words would be considered to be the same on the phonemic level. On the phonetic level, however, the *p* in *pin* is aspirated whereas the *p* in *spin* is unaspirated. If the focus is on the general, abstract or 'broad' sound level, which is the phonemic level here, then there is only one *p* sound in the English language. But if the focus is on the specific, concrete or 'narrow' level, which is the phonetic level here, then there are at least two different sounds present — namely *p* in *pin* and *p* in *spin*, where *p* is aspirated and *p* is unaspirated. In fact, the *p* too will always be different in phonetic detail each time it is pronounced in different contexts, but we can generalize all the specific occurrences of *p* as *p*.

Similarly, a musical tone is a generalized abstraction of many specific events. The frequency of the tone B, for example, will not be the same for any two occurrences of the tone. The cycle of a rhythm does not exactly equal the length of another cycle of the same rhythm, when time is viewed in terms of fractions of a second. Let us now proceed to the word or sentence level.

Consider the following Garhwali sentences:

(1) *wēn ábimanyu ni mār saki*
'He could not kill Abhimanyu'
(2) *wē se ábimanyu ni marḗ sakē*
'Abhimanyu could not be killed by him'
(3) *wēn ábimanyu tãi ni mār saki*
'He couldn't kill Abhimanyu'
(4) *wēn ábimanyu ki hatya ni kar saki*
'He couldn't do the assasination of Abhimanyu'
(5) *ábimanyu ki hatya wē se ni hwē saki*
'Abhimanyu's assasination could not be done by him'
(6) *ábimanyu wēn ni mār saki*
'He could not kill Abhimanyu'
(7) *ábimanyu wē se ni marḗ sakḗ*
'Abhimanyu could not be killed by him'
(8) *ábimanyu ni marḗ sakḗ wē se*
'Abhimanyu could not be killed by him'
(9) *wēn ni mār saki ábhimanyu tãi*
'He could not kill Abhimanyu'
(10) *ábimanyu tãi ni mār saki wēn*
'He could not kill Abhimanyu'
(11) *wē se ábimanyu ni marḗ*
'Abhimanyu could not be killed by him'
(12) *ábimanyu wē se ni marḗ*
'Abhimanyu could not be killed by him'

Here all twelve sentences give us the same broad information that 'someone failed to kill Abhimanyu'. If we take into consideration the specific details of each sentence, however, then each sentence differs from every other. For example, (1) is active and (2) is passive in terms of their grammatical formation. Sentence (12) is passive, but does not use the 'ability' verb *sak* 'can'. Sentence (3) has the particularizing postposition *tãi* after *ábimanyu*. Sentences (4) and (5) have the noun *hatya* 'assasination' with the verb *kar* 'do' and *ho* 'become, happen, take place (in the word *hwē*)'. Sentence (6) has a different word order than (1). Nevertheless, all these twelve sentences have some items in common which yield the same information. The subject is the same pronoun *wē*; the action or verb is about 'killing' and the person directly or indirectly related to the verb is *ábimanyu*; the same negative *ni* occurs in all the sentences.

The level which comes after the 'sentence', on a progressive scale, is the 'discourse'. A 'discourse' may be a poem, a story, a dialogue between two or more persons, etc. The *ábimanyu* story can be seen as a long discourse. We had the singers repeat this story several times both musically and non-musically, and although all versions tell the same story, each version differs from the others in both musical and non-musical features. The extent to which all versions are the same is due to the following broad components which are found in all versions of the story.

(a) Arjuna, the father of Abhimanyu and the third Pāṇḍava brother, leaves the capital to fight an enemy.

(b) The Kauravas, the evil-minded cousins of Arjuna, send a letter to Yudhiṣṭhira, the oldest among the Pāṇḍava brothers.

(c) Yudhiṣṭhira reads the letter, which is a challenge to take part in a war called *cakra-vyūha*. Yudhiṣṭhira is dismayed, because only Arjuna knows the rules by which this particular war is fought, and Arjuna is not at home.

(d) Abhimanyu, who is a teenage son of Arjuna, comes to see his uncle Yudhiṣṭhira.

(e) He tells Yudhiṣṭhira that when he was in the womb of his mother Subhadrā, his father Arjuna told her how to fight this particular war (which is fought in 7 fortresses or strategic circles). He had heard all the details of this war except those concerning the seventh fortress or circle. He missed this last because his mother (Subhadrā) fell asleep just as Arjuna had finished describing the first six circles.

(f) It is finally decided that Abhimanyu will destroy the first six circles which have been made by the Kauravas to trap and destroy the Pāṇḍavas and their forces. The seventh will be destroyed by the powerful Bhīma, the second among the five Pāṇḍava brothers.

(g) Before leaving for the battle, Abhimanyu meets with his grandmother Kuntī. She gives him a sacred thread for his wrist. In accordance with her blessing, the sacred thread will protect Abhimanyu as long as he keeps it on his wrist.

(h) On his way to the battlefield he meets Krishna, who is in the disguise of a priest. Krishna knows that Abhimanyu is an incarnation of a demon and will kill him (Krishna). So the disguised Krishna asks Abhimanyu to give him the thread. Abhimanyu gives the thread away, and Krishna is satisfied that he will no longer enjoy its protection.

(i) Abhimanyu goes into the battlefield and destroys the first six circles.

(j) The cunning Jayadratha is hiding on the seventh circle, and kills Abhimanyu by foul means.

(k) Arjuna returns home, hears the bad news, and goes to the battlefield, where he kills Jayadratha.

Now consider the two versions of the Abhimanyu story as they are given in Daunr Text 1 and Daunr Text 2. These two texts contain all the broad components from (a) to (k) in their evolutionary or progressive order. In this regard the two versions could be said to be the same story. However, the two versions can also be seen to differ when they are considered from the point of view of their narrow components. The reader will see in Daunr Text 1 and Daunr Text 2, that the sentences, intonations and rhythms all differ. For instance, the tempo in the beginning of Daunr Text 1 is fast, while it is very slow in the beginning of Daunr Text 2.

A more interesting case was observed in Dhol Text 5 and Dhol Text 6. These two texts are from the same singers. The two versions incorporate all the broad components from (a) to (k), but not exactly in their progressive or evolutionary order. The broad components (g) and (h) of the story occur between (i) and (k). That is, the lead singer forgot to tell the (g) and (h) parts of the story after he told the (f) part. When Abhimanyu was killed the lead singer recalled that he could not have been killed if he had had the sacred thread on his wrist (given by his grandmother for his protection). This sacred thread had been taken away by Krishna before Abhimanyu had left for the battlefield.

The device of 'recall' is well-known in storytelling, and in fact is common in all discourse. The story tellers or writers may employ this 'recall' device on purpose in order to introduce a 'surprise' element. Even at the sentence level, a speaker can employ the 'recall' device when he forgets an item. For example, *wēn* may have occurred at the end instead of at the beginning of sentence (10) above because of 'recall'. Sentences in normal discourse can become very complex because of recall. The written discourse which we see in print has usually been edited. Natural spoken sentences are loaded with many features which are eliminated in edited language. Recall is one such feature which may be discarded in an edited discourse.

Sometimes a broad component of a story may not be overt. There is then a covert or 'suggested' indication of such a component. For instance, in Dholki Text 3 the broad component that King Ugrasena had a queen named Pavanarekhā is given overtly in the sentence *tai rāja kī chayī parbhu jo bhagibāna jī chayī rānī pabanarekha*. On the other hand, in Dholki Text 4 we are not told overtly that Pavanarekhā was the queen of King Ugrasena. We rather as hearers reconstruct this information from the sentence *ik din samai bod pabanrekha ji swāmi* . . . 'one day Pavanarekhā says "O husband!" . . .'. The term of address 'husband' suggests that Pavanarekhā is the queen. Note that the singers of Dholki Text 3 are different from those of Dholki Text 4.

When the singers differ, their versions of the same story also differ. This is partly because of their choice of words. One example of such individual stylistic differences occurs in Dholki Texts 3 and 4. The word for 'God' is *bhagbān* in Dholki Text 3 and *nāraiṇ* in Dholki Text 4. There are also phonetic variations in different occurrences of the same word: e.g. *bhagibāna* 'God' in the pronunciation of Kundan (the singer of Dholki Text 3), and *bhagobāna* or *bhagubāna* 'God' in the pronunciation of Bachandas (the singer of Dhol Text 2). The linguistic aspects in the grammatical sense will be discussed next.

Linguistic Abnormalities

How the association of language with music occurs can be considered from an evolutionary point of view. There are two evolutionary formations which we can observe in Garhwali music. In one formation the normal language is converted into a fixed form known as the poetic language. Then the poetic form is converted into a musical form. This evolution can be shown by means of arrows as:

Formation I: Language → Poetry → Song

It is also possible for language to skip the middle stage of development. That is, normal language can be directly converted into a musical form without being first converted into poetry. This second manner of evolution can be represented as:

Formation II: Language → Song

The Dholki texts are an example of Formation I, and all other texts given here are examples of Formation II.

In folk music such as Garhwali singing, where improvisation plays an important role, no part of the music ever receives a permanent form. The Dholki texts, for example, never appear twice with exactly the same words and tones. It is possible, however, to edit or reconstruct most Dholki texts as a poetic form. Other texts, with very few exceptions, cannot be reconstructed as something which could be called a poetic form. The other texts sound poetic to the hearer because of their musical form. They exemplify the instant conversion of language into a musical form and could be called the product of synchronic evolution. The Dholki texts, in contrast, are the result of diachronic evolution. (In both kinds of evolution, the listener has the competence to edit or reconstruct the original normal language version from the language present in the song text.)

Language itself goes through these two phases of evolution — diachronic and synchronic. A theory and method of synchronic or descriptive evolution of the sentence is given in Chandola (1975).

The point to be emphasized here is that language changes considerably, in the evolutionary sense, when it goes from normal language to musical language. Here we will give some examples of grammatical changes found in these song texts. Most of these changes can be observed by comparing the song text version with its following language text.

Consider the sentences of Dholki Text 3. It begins with the words *mathura ma rãida*. The singers repeat these and other words wholly or partially several times, before the sentence is completed with two more words — *r̄aja ukrasaina*. The basic sentence can be reconstructed as *mathura ma rãida rāja ukrasaina* 'There lives King Ugrasena in Mathura'. The additional words *parbhu, jo, bhagibāna*, and *ji* are possible in this sentence only because of the musical context, and the idiosyncratic choices made by the singers. The repetition of the items of the actual basic sentence, plus the idiosyncratic choices of the singers, evolve a new language pattern which is available only in a song text form.

We have seen above that the original normal sentence *mathura ma rãida rāja ukrasaina* has been surrounded by items which could be considered redundant. Such a case can be called *overestimation* of information. There can also be a case of *underestimation*. Consider the sentence in Dhol Text 2, *durṇā jī kā pāsa jālo drōdhana kā pāśa*. This sentence would be reconstructed in normal language as *durṇā ji ka pāsa jālo, drōdhan ka pās jālo* '(Bhagban) will go to Droṇa (and he) will go to Duryodhana'. The verb *jālo* 'will go' is missing after the phrase *drōdhana kā pāśa* 'to Duryodhana' in the song text. This kind of ellipsis is not possible in normal language. From the point of view of normal language, this ellipsis is a case of *underestimation* of information. The underestimated sentence is reconstructed on the basis of the identical items it shares with the immediately preceding sentence. The preceding sentence in this case is *durṇā jī kā pāsa jālo*. Both sentences have the items *kā* and *pāsa* preceded by a noun class (given in one as *durnā*, in the other as *drōdhana*) which has an identical grammatical function in each sentence.

There are both musical and psychological reasons for the singers' partial or complete repetition of sentences. Musically, the singers aim at keeping the intonational and rhythmic patterns at a set level. The emphasis on the musical aspect is so great that the grammatical and sound patterns of the words may be altered. Psychologically, the singers face the problem of remembering the words of the text. The repetition of words or of a sentence offers them some time to recall the next sentence.

An example of a gramatical change is the word *pā̃suṛi* in Part III of Dhol Text 1. This word, which is feminine in the normal language, appears in this song text as masculine (as is indicated by its being preceded by the masculine adjective marker *ka* rather than the normal feminine *ki*).

In addition to gender changes, some grammatical categories may occur in the song text which do not occur in the normal language. One such case is the historical future tense of the verbs. The verb *jālo* 'will be' in Dhol Text 2 Part I actually functions as the historical future, and means 'went'. There may also be a historical progressive future, such as *laginī holī* 'will be starting' in Daunr Text 1, stanza (2), which means there 'was in the process of taking place'. Notice in the same text the use of *lagī holī* 'will have started' in the sense of 'has started', and compare it with the normal *lagī gaye* in the preceding stanza of the same text, where it means 'has started'. Other texts also provide many examples of the use of the future in the sense of past.

The idiosyncratic words may occur between two words which are normally not separated by other words. For example, the compound verb construction *hwē jain* is split by the idiosyncratic word *rē* in the first sentence of Daunr Text 2. In the second sentence of this text we find *santānī rē aulāda* where *rē* splits the attributive adjective (*santānī*) and the noun it specifies (*aulāda*). The insertion of a word such as *rē* can be done in this manner only in song texts. Words like *bhagibāna*, *parbhu*, and *jo*, in Dholki Text 3, which are inserted several times between the items of the sentence *mathura mā̃ rāida rājā ukrasaina,* are in the same category as *rē*.

A few monosyllabic idiosyncratic words like *rē* may split a single word, although this is very rare in these song texts. One example (not included in the texts given in this book) is from the singer of Daunr Texts 1-2. The word *arjun* 'Arjuna' appears as *arijana* in the song text. (It has appeared also as *arī rē jana*.) This is a case of vowel insertion (*svarabhakti*) as well as of grammatical insertion, which is found only in the song text context. Cases of vowel insertion are very common and the reader may easily find examples by comparing a song text version with its language text version. For instance, the normal *bhagbān* appears in the song texts as *bhagībāna*, *bhagūbāna*, *bhagōbāna*, *bhagabāna*, etc.

Another alteration, in addition to vowel insertion, is that the length of a vowel may be increased to an extraordinary degree. For example, in Hurki Text 2 the final *ā* of the word *jōgamāyā* is lengthened to an extent impossible in a normal context. The normally short vowels may also be lengthened: e.g. the short vowel *i* in the normal *meri* 'my', is lengthened in *merī* in the Hurki Text. In singing, any short vowel can be made a long vowel in this manner. Examples of this can be found by comparing a song text version with its following language text version.

A word ending in a consonant can have the short vowel *a* added to it, and this vowel can then be lengthened from *a* to the long vowel *ā*, which can be prolonged as long as wished. For example, the normal phonetic shape of the word *jalā* is *jal* 'water'. It evolves from *jal* to *jala* to *jalā*. The middle stage *jala*, however, is bypassed here. This change affects the syllabic shape of the word. The normal syllabic shape of *jal* is CVC (where C=consonant, and V=vowel). Its form in singing has become CVCV, where the last consonant *l* is sung with the last vowel, giving the word two syllables instead of one. That is, the consonants are redistributed in their syllabic division.

One interesting phonological phenomenon is that one of the singers can join the other singer from any non-initial syllable of a non-inital word of a stanza of the preceding singer. Consider the word *sewāṛi* 'salutation' where the subordinate singer joins the lead singer by singing the last two syllables *wāṛi* (Dhol Text 5). See also in Daunr Text 1, stanza (2) where the subordinate singer joins the lead singer by starting with the last syllable *lī* of the word *holī* 'will be'. Such a phenomenon is only possible in Garhwali in a musicolinguistic context such as this. There are, however, constraints on the kinds of sounds with which a singer can join the preceding singer. These constraints are governed by the phonetic constraints of the normal language. For instance, in Part III of Dhol Text 1, it can be predicted that the subordinate singer can under no circumstances join the lead singer from the syllable *ṛa* of the word *caupaṛā* or *caupṛō*. This is so because in Garhwali no word can start with the sound *ṛ*.

An abnormal range of vocabulary is also noticeable. We have

observed very archaic words — words totally absent from the normal language — such as *kāgaḷi* 'letter' instead of the normal *ciṭṭhi* (see Dhol and Daunr texts), *netar* 'tears' instead of *ā̃su* (see Dhol Text 5), *kāruṇ* 'crying' instead of *roṇu* (see Dhol Text 5), etc. On the other hand, very recent loans have also entered into the song text vocabulary through normal language usage. For example, words like *iskūl* 'school' and *māsṭar* 'schoolmaster, teacher' have occurred in some of the *Abhimanyu* story versions (not given in this book). The recent loans are from English and have been completely absorbed into the normal language. Thus, we see the extreme range of vocabulary — from the oldest to the newest — in these song texts.

This use of recent loan words presents a sharp contrast to the *Mahābhārata* stories in other Indo-Aryan languages, e.g. those written in Hindi by sophisticated writers. The sophisticated writer never uses English loans when dealing with a religious theme like the *Mahābhārata* stories. For example, the words normally expected in a Hindi *Mahābhārata* story would be *pāṭhśālā* 'school' and *guru* 'teacher' in place of the two loan words shown above. The folk artist, on the other hand, has no awareness of loans as loans.

The folk singer seems to spontaneously blend not only vocabulary from different linguistic sources, but even different languages. Consider Part I of Hurki Text 1 where the language is a form of medieval Hindi known as *sadhukkaṛī* 'the language of the sādhu' (the term *sādhu* means 'saint'). This hybrid form of Hindi originated with traveling saints like Kabīr and Nānak, who, as they wandered, added words from the different linguistic regions of northern India — Panjabi, Rajasthani, Bhojpuri, etc. — to a base of the Braj and Khari dialects of Hindi. Part I of Hurki Text 1, a prayer to the god *narsiṅ* (Sanskrit *nṛsiṁha*), is in *sadhukkaṛī* Hindi.

While there are historical reasons for the hybrid *sadhukkaṛī* form of some prayers and benedictions, the Hindi *sadhukkaṛī* becomes even more hybridized when it reaches the Garhwali region. For example, the occurrence of the Garhwali word *kwī* 'anyone' in Part III of Daunr Text 1 increases the hybridization of the text. Occasionally a dialogue or monologue may occur in modern standard Hindi-Urdu. For example, in the middle of Dhol Text 2 (not included in this book) when Arjuna learns of the murder of his son Abḥimanyu, he takes a vow which is partly in Hindi-Urdu: *agar mãi ne dusṭī mār diyā to ṭhīk ho gayā hai* 'if I killed the rogue then it has become alright'. Some Sanskrit words also appear in hybrid forms, such as *siri gaṇesāy nam* for the Sanskrit *śrī gaṇēśāya namaḥ* 'salutation to Lord Gaṇeśa'. The mixture of standard Hindi-Urdu and hybrid Sanskrit, however, can occur in normal Garhwali as well as in its musical form.

Meter

A performance of Garhwali drumming music always begins and ends with loud drumming, i.e., drumming which is high in amplitude. The lead singer starts the language text after a few rhythmic cycles at the beginning of the performance, and the drumming then diminishes and becomes light (low in amplitude) or there may be no drumming at all. Loud drumming is very rarely played simultaneous with the singing of a song text. When this occurs, the last one or two sentences of the immediately preceding text are repeated. Such repetition is usually possible only with those texts which are musically metric. A text is musically metric if it can be measured in a system of regular pulsation or time units occurring in a cycle. Such time units are normally known as beats. The texts may or may not be linguistically metric. The linguistic meter is determined by a system of some regular phonetic quantity or quality.

There is no folk verse built on a phonetic quantitative basis in Garhwali. In this sense, Garhwali verse could be called 'improvised free verse'. The basis of the Dholki texts is qualitative rather than quantitative. These texts are based on 'rime'. That is, the last syllables of the last words of the lines have the same sounds. In Dholki Texts Nos. 1-2, for instance, we see a repetition of the sequence *ānād*. In the long narrative stories improvised by the drummers, it is not possible for them to produce instant metric lines. The Dholki texts, which are very short compared to the non-Dholki texts, are memorized, and are composed in riming couplets. Very rarely, the non-Dholki drummers insert short rimed texts into the middle of a long narrative, e.g. a short dance song in praise of the goddess Kāli. It is the length of a song text, not the use of a particular drum, which is responsible for the presence or absence of rime. Shorter texts tend to have rime, while longer ones do not.

These texts, which do not have any linguistic meter, still give the listener a false sense of hearing a regular meter when they are sung by a drummer. This false sense which we can call 'metricalness' is due to the fact that the text is accompanied by drumming. Drumming is a strictly metered phenomenon in both a qualitiative and a quantitative sense; e.g. a rhythm always recurs with the same cyclic length and strokes. Thus the musical meter is able to compensate for the absence of a linguistic meter.

Similar musical intonation also renders a feeling of linguistic metricalness. For example, in Dhol Text 1 the subordinate singer (the Damau player) sings the vowel *ā* in the tone of C or D at the end of every line (except in the first line where the vowel is *o*). This vowel *ā* has no meaning outside the musical context, and is translated by ϕ (zero) in the song texts. Such words and syllables can be called 'musical' words, meaning that they serve a musical function rather than contributing to the meaning of a sentence. The function of the 'musical' word *ā*, in this case, is to render metricalness to the text. This pattern is seen wherever the part of the subordinate singer occurs (indicated by ↓ to ↑ in the song text).

In some texts, metricalness is rendered by the subordinate singer's repetition of a line. For example, in Part III of Dhol Text 1, the subordinate singer repeats the line *baiṭhi cauparau/cauparā*. This linguistic repetition is paralleled by rhythmic and tonal regularities.

The degree of metricalness varies from text to text. Those texts which have a very low degree of metricalness are marked by a very low frequency of linguistic participation by the subordinate singer. For example, in Part II of Dhol Text 2, the subordinate singer does not sing. We have called this part a 'prose recitation', as is indicated in the song texts. Very infrequently, the subordinate singer may join the lead singer near the end with a vowel marked by a single tone which is prolonged until the lead singer begins another line. We see this situation in Part I of Dhol Text 5, where the subordinate singer joins in at line (3) and prolongs the vowel *ā* of the last syllable *rā* which was uttered by the lead singer.

Prose recitation, in comparison with other kinds of singing, is marked by the presence of fewer tones and the absence of any regular rhythms. For example, in Part I of Dhol Text 5 we notice only three tones: B, B♭ and C (excepting a slight touch of G in line (2)). The drumming which follows a line or group of lines in a prose recitation may be a plain sequence of two kinds of strokes in a short cycle of two beats. (See Dhol R 10 and Damau R 10 for examples). Sometimes there is no drumming during the prose recitation, as we see in Part II of Dhol Text 2.

Due to the need for rhyming, another major pattern is displayed in Garhwali folk songs. In this pattern, the first line of every couplet of a song is related to the second line not thematically or semantically, but only metrically. This is exemplified in the *ghasyari* Text (see Appendix). In the Language Text of the *ghasyari* Song Text we see that *bā̃kōr* of (2a) rhymes with *cakōr* of (2b), and *cirāg* of (3a) rhymes with *phirāg* of (3b). However, the meaning or sense of (2a) has no connection with that of (2b). That is, (2a) and (2b) are not part of a coherent linguistic discourse as far as the unity of their subject matter is concerned. The same is true of (3a) and (3b) or any other couplets of this song (the remaining couplets of the song are not given in the text).

Compare this style with that of a children's song of English like

One two
Buckle my shoe

where the major motivation for the occurence of 'two' is that it rhymes with 'shoe'.

This pattern may occur in all Garhwali songs except those which are auspicious, shamanistic, or ballads (with minor exceptions).

Another characteristic of the *ghasyari* Song Text is that a linguistic meter may be accompanied by a musical meter which redistributes the lines in a way differing from the distribution of the linguistic meter. The linguistic meter is based on the normal language (spoken) version, not on the version which has been influenced by being set to music. Both types of meter occur in a single text. For example, Part I and Part III of the *ghasyari* Song Text are sung rhythmically (i.e. with a musical meter), while Part II is not. In terms of the linguistic meter, Part II and the first portion of Part III through the word *cakōra* make one couplet, as is shown in (2a) and (2b) of the Language Text version of the *ghasyari* Song Text. That is, the couplet, which is linguistically determined (by the rime), is formed from all of Part II and part of Part III. The boundary between Part II and Part III, on the other hand, is determined by a difference in musical meter. Thus, we clearly see here that musical meter overlaps the boundary of linguistic meter, and linguistic and musical meter may be independent of each other in a text.

It has been said earlier that Garhwali folk verse is not based on a linguistic (phonetic) quantity. The Language Text of the *ghasyari* Song Text demonstrates this fact, as do the Dholki Texts (note that the *ghasyari* song may or may not be accompanied by the Dholki, Hurki, or Daunr). An apparent contradiction to this assertion that Garhwali folk verse is not based on phonetic quantity is seen in the Song Text (not the Language Text) version of the *ghasyari* song. We see in this text the following syllabic distribution derived from the musical version.

dhāra ma ka lāla maṇī dai khai ja pāta ma = 14 syllables
o b̃āsuḷi b̃ākōra = 7 syllables
tera bānā ṭaparā̃dū ḍā̃ḍa si cakōra = 14 syllables

The same syllabic scheme of 14, 7, 14 occurs for the musical version of the Language Text version. Thus, one may be led to believe that in some Garhwali folk songs phonetic quantity may be relevant in metrics. Actually, however, this is a version which is based on the musical version rather than on the normal language. Furthermore, this syllabic scheme is a chance occurrence here, as it does not appear in the other couplets of this song (not given in the Song Text).

This apparent phonetic regularity also appears if we write this song in Devanagari script. This script adds an inherent vowel *a*, not present in the spoken language, after consonants. In Devanagari script the Garhwali word *dhār* becomes *dhāra*, as it is in the song text version. The script versions of these songs are not relevant, however, as the singers are not aware of the intricacies of the writing system. Any justification of meter on the basis of writing conventions is therefore a teleological approach.

Final Remarks

We now need to find those universals that determine the patterns of music and language in the song texts. This is possible only when large scale comparative studies in musicolinguistics are pursued. Our aim must be to unfold the inner principles that guide or motivate the musicolinguistic acts of the performers, without theoretical or methodological biases. No act can be understood in isolation. An act is merely an effect of one or more causes which may be social, psychological, physical, physiological, etc. That is, real in-depth studies would be based on the principle of cause and effect — the evolutionary approach.

Language and music are vital parts of any society. Since each part affects the other in an organic system, musicolinguistics must assert its proper place in social and behavioral studies through its use of scientific tools rather than the commonly adopted esthetic or artistic approaches. Here such an attempt is made. Some parts of this attempt will undoubtedly turn out to be speculative when further research has been done by other social and behavioral scientists. The question is this: How do we encourage more research? One way to create an interest in such studies is by academic departments of anthropology, linguistics or sociology offering a course on "Music, Language and Society." Such a course could easily be incorporated into the regular programs of these departments.

The most natural interaction of music and language is observed in folk music. The smaller folk cultures are rapidly being replaced by the major cultures. Scholars in linguistics and ethnomusicology, as well as folklore, must bear a responsibility for the academic preservation of these dying folk cultures. This work is an effort in that direction.

ILLUSTRATIONS

1 The Dhol: Stroke N. The left hand slap ready to strike the drum face.

2 The Dhol: Stroke V. The right hand fingers in snap position (holding the stick) ready to slide down the drum face.

3 The Dhol: Strokes T and O. The stick strikes and remains placed in the center of the right face while the left hand slap is ready to strike the left face (corner).

4 The Dhol: Strokes L and M (rotating). The bent knee is ready to strike the right face after the stick stroke.

1

2

3

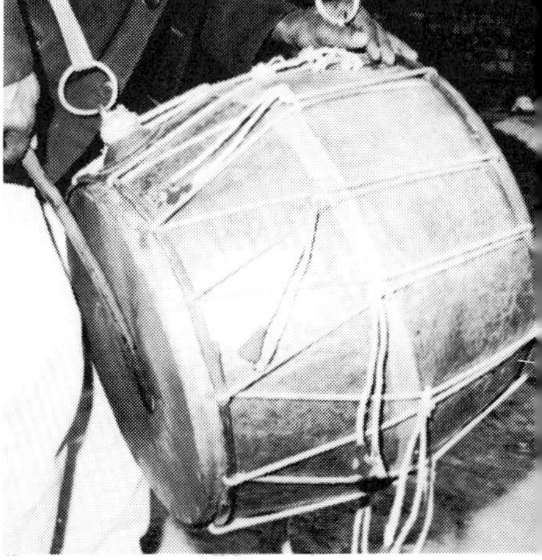

4

5

6

5 The Dhol: Strokes L[1] and O (rotating). The stick strikes on (or slightly below) the center, while the slap strikes between the corner and center of the left face (the right face is resting on the right knee).

6 The Dhol (left) and the Damau (right) players. The Dhol Stroke is O. The Damau Stroke is M.

7 The Dholki: Stroke K.

8 The Dholki: Stroke O.

7

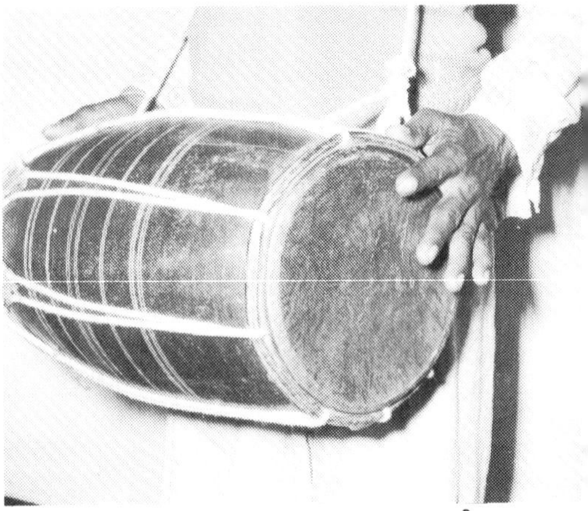

8

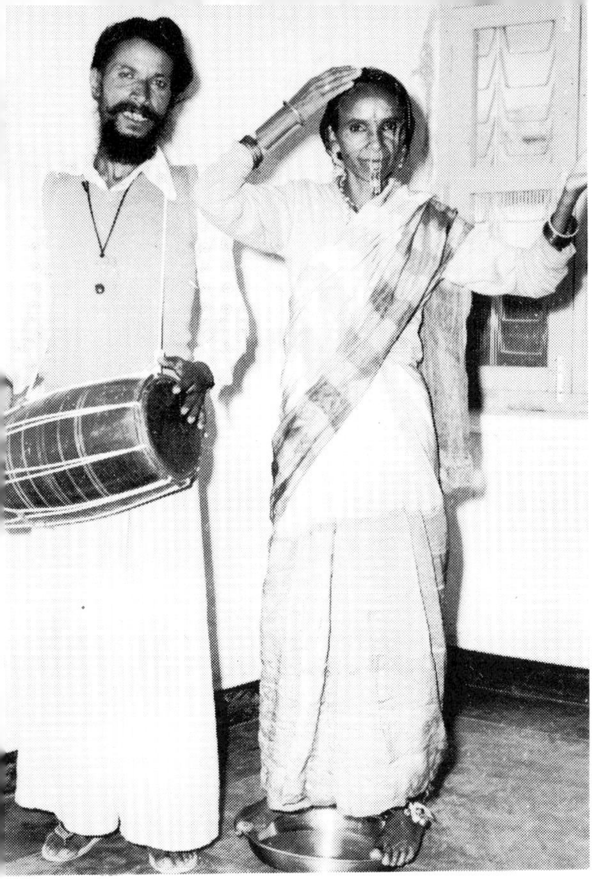

9

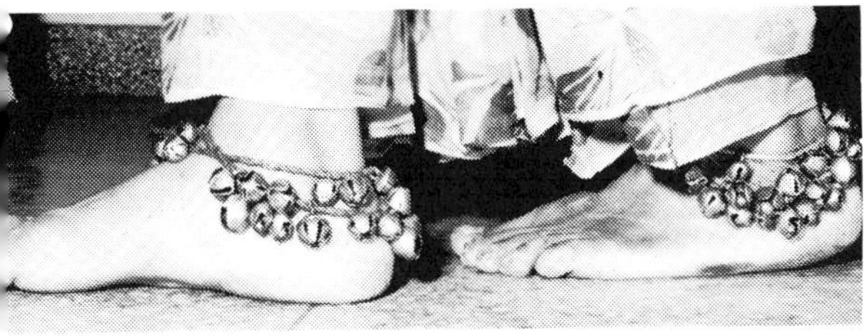

10

9 The Dholki player (man) and the dancer (woman). The Dholki Stroke is M. The woman with the Ghungrus tied around her ankles is dancing on the rim of a large metal plate which rotates under her feet.

10 The Ghungrus: Strokes M and N (rotating). This woman is dancing on the floor. The anklebells (Ghungrus) are clearly seen here around her ankles.

11 The Daunr: Stroke L. The drum is held between the knees.

12 The Daunr: Stroke V.

11

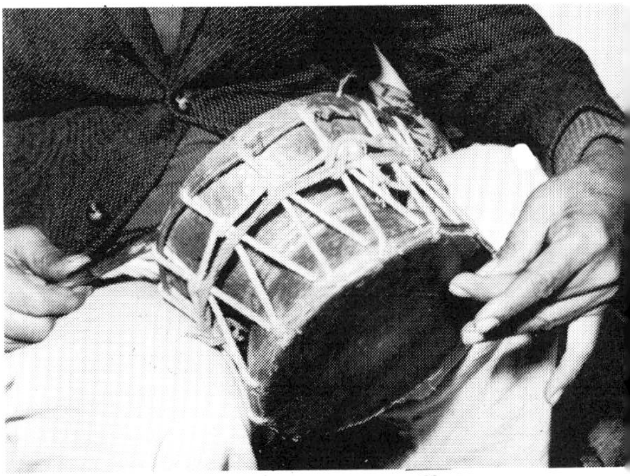

12

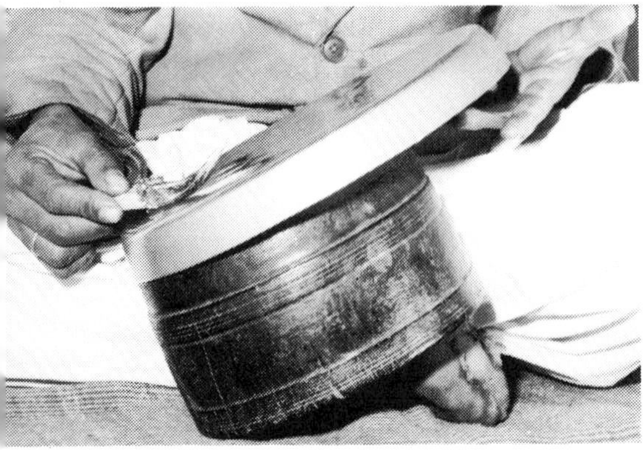

13

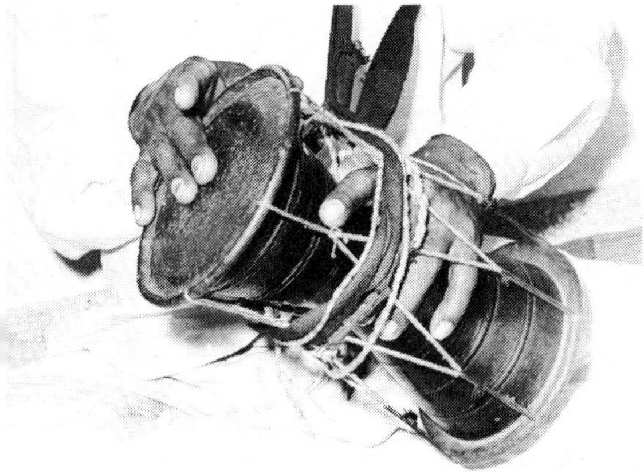

13 The Thali-Pathu: Stroke M. The Pathu's right bottom is placed on the floor and the left bottom is on the left foot of the player (who is sitting cross-legged). The Thali's right side is resting on the right top rim of the Pathu and the left side is held by the No. 3 finger of the left hand.

14 The Hurki: Stroke T.

15 The Thali player (left), the Hurki player (center) and the author (right). The Hurki stroke is M. The right bottom of the Thali is on the floor and the left one is resting on the left foot of the player. The Thali strokes are M and N, rotating.

14

15

APPENDIX

Texts

The song texts do not show the linguistic tones of the words. The tones have been marked in the language text versions of each song text. The language text represents the normal pronunciation of the singers, where normal means 'non-musical' (spoken). In a song text version, the ɸ (zero) represents a small pause; a comma represents a pause longer than zero; and a semi-colon represents a pause longer than a comma. In the language version, the symbol 'ɸ' (zero) indicates that there is no translation for that item. See the chapter 'Textual Aspects' for a further explanation of these texts. It should be noted that the texts given here are only a small portion of our total recorded texts, and have been selected as representative samples. The text listed under the name of a lead drum includes the portions of both the lead and the subordinate drums and singers of the team.

The use of arrows in the song texts is as follows: The '↑' begins the portion of the lead singer. The '↓' begins the portion of the subordinate singer. The '↕' is the part common to both the lead and the subordinate singer. For example, in Dhol Text 1 Part I (1) the lead singer begins at the syllable *ā* and continues by himself through the syllable *tha*, when he is joined by the subordinate singer on the syllable *ya*, as is indicated by the arrows. After the syllable *yē* the lead singer stops singing, and the subordinate singer continues by himself for the remainder of (1).

Sometimes the subordinate singer joins the lead singer with a slightly different version of the portion being sung. This difference may be in terms of tones, time and syllables, or even words. To indicate this, this portion is shown below the main song text line. For example, in Dholki Text 3 the word *bhagibāna* of the lead singer is sung concurrently by the subordinate singer with a different distribution of time and tones, and with the addition of the word *jī*. This is why the portion *bhagibāna jī* of the subordinate singer, with its time and tones, is given below the main line (note the '↓' before it which indicates that this is the portion of the subordinate singer). The lead singer then stops with the syllable *na* of the word *bhagibana* and the subordinate singer continues on alone as is indicated by another '↓', now on the main line.

Similarly, the lead singer can also join the subordinate singer in the same way. For an example, see Dhol Text 2 Part I where the subordinate singer is still singing the syllable *yā* when the lead singer joins him with the two syllables *dwā* and *ri* of the word *dwārikā*. The subordinate singer then stops at the syllable *kā* of the same word, as is indicated by the arrows.

The word 'drumming' in a song text indicates 'loud drumming'. The absence of this word indicates that singing is continuing, with or without light drumming.

The abbreviation hon. = honorific particle.

Dhol Text 1

Part I.

(1) Ab - - Ab Bb Ab ϕ ϕ C C C D E D E E C D D - E - D - D E - D -
↑
ā - - - - - ϕ ϕ pa r bhu ja ba - pa ra ga ṭa hwē- j̃ā - dī - nā - - tha -

A C ^A C ^A C C - - - - - - - C - - - - - - - - - C - - - -
↕ ↓
ya - - - ye - - - - - - - ā - - - - - - - - - ō - - - -

(2) C C D - E E D C D C A ^A C D - C C A A C - D E - ^A C -
↑
bha ga bā - nu - - bi snu - - ca yō - - - - au - - tā - - rā -

D - - - - - - D - - - - - - - -
↕ ↓
yē - - - - - - ā - - - - - - - -

(3) C - - D E E D E D D E G D - D - C A ᴬC ᴬC ᴬC -
ye - - bis nu au - tā - ra - - tyā - ro - - - yā - - -

C - - - - - - - - - - C - - - - - - - - - - - -
ye - - - - - - - - - - ā - - - - - - - - - - - -

(4) C C D - E E D C C C D - C A D - C C D - D C A C D C - D -
bha ga bā - na - - pir tha bī - - - yā - jal - mā - - - - - hwē - - nā -

D - - - - - D - - - - - - - - - - - - - - -
yē - - - - - ā - - - - - - - - - - - - - - -

```
(5)  C  C  E  D  C  A  C  C  C  D  -  D  E  -  D  -  C  A  A  C  A  C
     ↑pi r tha bī  -  -  ja  l  mā hwē  -  na nā  -  tha  -  -  -  ā  -  -  -

     C  -  -  -  -  -  -  -    -  -  -  -  -  -  -  C  -  -  -  -  -  -  -  -  -  -  -  -  -  .
     ↕                       ↓
     yē -  -  -  -  -  -  -    -  -  -  -  -  -  -  ā  -  -  -  -  -  -  -  -  -  -  -  -  -

(6)  B♭ A♭ C  D  -  E  D  -  A  -  C  D  -  E  D  ϕ  A  C  -  D  C  -
     ↑
     hē  -  tu mā  -  rā  -  -  cau  -  bi sū  -  a  ba  ϕ  tā  -  -  rā  -  -

     D  -  -  -  -  -  -  -    -  -  -  -  -  -  -  -  -  -  D  -  -  -  -  -  -  -  -  -  -  -
     ↕                       ↓
     yē -  -  -  -  -  -  -    -  -  -  -  -  -  -  -  -  -  ā  -  -  -  -  -  -  -  -  -  -  -
```

(7) ↑ A - G G G G E D, E♭ D, C D, - C - C D - D E♭ - D, C D A C, A C, -

ō - ka lu kā la mā -, ja l, mā -, - lē - nyā nā - rā - - -, ya na - -, - -, -

C - - - - - C ↓ -

↕ ā - - - - - yē -

(8) ↑ C C C D D - D - E - D C, D - D E, - D C, A C A, C - E,

gha ru gha ru kī - yā - pū - jā -, bī - lē -, - nā -, - - -, tu - ma

D - - - - - D -

↕ nā - - - - - yē - - - - - ↓ - - - - - - - - - - - - - - - - - - -

Text

Part II.

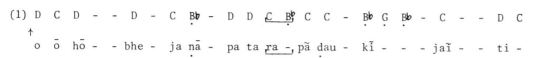

(1) D C D - - D - C B♭ - D D C B♭ C C - B♭ G B♭ - C - - D C
↑
o ō hō - - bhe - ja nā - pa ta ra -, pã dau - kī - - - jaĩ - - ti -

B♭ G ↓ - - D C B♭ - G - - -
↕
yā - - - mā̃ - - - jā - - -

(2) G B♭ B♭ C D, C B♭ C C C, C - B♭ C - C - - - D D C B♭ B♭ C, C B♭ C B♭ - - ;
↑
jãi - jãi - tī - -, pa ta ra, mā - li khyũ - ca - - - dur yō - -, dha na kaũ-, ko -, - - ;

B♭ - B♭ C - B♭ C C C C B♭ -, B♭ B♭ - C - C C C - C B♮ C D B C C C B♭,
↑
hē - bhu lā - - dha r ma rā ja -, i nū - kā - ma ka ryā - nā -, pā̃ cī -bhai - tu ma,

```
B♭ - B♭ C B♭ C C C C C D - C B♭ C D C B♭ C C C C B♭ C D B♭,
cha - taũ - -, du r pa di lhē-, - ka -, bhu lā - -, dharma rā ja tu mu - -,

B♭ B♭ G - - C C D - B♭ - C - C - - - - - - - - -
ha ti nā - - pu ra ma - ai - nā - ye - - - - - - - - -      jācnī Drumming
```

Part III

```
(1)  1  2  3  4  5  6 | 1  2  3  4  5  6 | 1  2  3  4  5  6 | 1  2  3  4  5  6
     F  G  -  -  -  - | A♭ G  -  -  -  - | A♭ G  -  F  A♭ - | G. -  -  -  -  -
   ↑
     o  hō -  -  -  - | hō -  -  -  -  - | bai thi - cau pa - | rā -  -  -  -  -

     A♭ G  G  A♭ F  F | G  -  -  -  G  G | A♭ G  -  F  A♭ G | G  -  G  -  -  -
   ↓                                 ↑~
     bai thi - cau - pa | rau- - - ū ki | bai thi- cau - pa | ra - ō - - -
```

1	2	3	4	5	6	1	2	3	4	5	6	1	2	3	4	5	6	1	2	3	4	5	6
↓ Ab	G	-	Ab	G	F	G	-	-	G	-	-	-	↑F	F	Ab	G	-	F	Ab	-	-	[GF]	[AbG]
bai	ṭhi	-	cau	-	pa	ṛā	-	-	ō	-	-	-	tu	na	ja	yī	-	bā	bū	-	-	[- -]	[- -]
Ab	G	-	Ab	G	F	G	-	-	F	G	G	Ab	-	G	F	Eb	F	G	-	Ab	G	F	G
↓ bai	ṭhi	-	cau	-	pa	ṛau	-	-	↑ ku	ṭha	ṛi	ban	-	dai	ka	rī	-	gai	-	nā	-	-	-
Ab	G	-	Ab	G	F	G	-	-	G	G	-	Ab	-	G	F	F	Eb	F	-	G	-	[AF]	[GF]
↓ bai	ṭhi	-	cau	-	pa	ṛā	-	-	↑ a	ba	-	yū̃	-	dwi	yī	bhā	-	yū̃	-	kī	-	[- -]	[- -]
Ab	G	-	Ab	G	F	G	-	-	G	G	G	F	F	-	Ab	-	G	G	-	-	A	[AG]	[GF]
↓ bai	ṭhi	-	cau	-	pa	ṛau	-	-	↑ yo	ba	la	ku	khe	-	lā	-	hū̃	dā	-	-	-	--	--

1	2	3	4	5	6	1	2	3	4	5	6	1	2	3	4	5	6	1	2	3	4	5	6
A♭	G	-	A♭	G	F	G	-	-	-	-	-	A♭	-	G	E♭	-	F	A♭	-	G	-	G	-
↓ bai	ṭhi	-	cau	-	pa	ṛau-	-	-	-	-	-	↑ hā	-	ra	jī	-	ta	kā	-dwai		-	pā̃	-
A♭	-	G	F	E♭	G	A♭	-	-	G	-	-	Drumming with six beats											
su	-	ṛi	khe-		la	lā	-	↕ -	-	-	-												

Language Text of Dhol Text 1
Note: The symbol 'ɸ' (zero) appears as the literal translation of a word to indicate that such a word has no possible context in the normal language, as it occurs only in singing.

Part I.

(1)
ā paŕbhu jáb pargaṭ hwē jā́di náth yā yē ā ō
ɸ lord! when manifest become have lord! ɸ ɸ ɸ ɸ
'Lord! when you have become manifest . . . '

(2)
bhagbānu bísnu ca yō autār yē ā
God's Viṣṇu is this incarnation ɸ ɸ
'then Viṣṇu is God's incarnation.'

(3)
yē bísnu autār tyāro yā yē ā
ɸ Viṣṇu incarnation your ɸ ɸ ɸ
'This is your Viṣṇu incarnation.'

(4)
bhagbān pirthabī ya jal mā hwēn yē ā
God! earth or water in became ɸ ɸ
'on earth and in water took place . . .'

(5)
pirthabi jal mā hwēn náth ā yē ā
earth water in became lord! ɸ ɸ ɸ
'on earth and in water took place . . . '

(6)
he túmara cáubisu abtār yē ā
ɸ your twenty-four incarnations ɸ ɸ
'Your twenty-four incarnations.'

(7)
o kalu kāl mā jal mā lenyā nārāyaṇa ā yē
ɸ Kali age in water in took Nārāyaṇa ɸ ɸ
'In the age of Kali, O Nārāyaṇa! You took place in water.'

(8)
gharu gharu kī yā pūja bi lén túmun ye
home home of ɸ worship too took you ɸ
'You acçepted the homage too from each and every home.'

Part II:
(1)
o ō hō bhejṇa patar pāḍau kī jā̃iti yā mā̃j
ɸ ɸ ɸ send letter Pāṇḍava of Jayantī ɸ in
'They send a letter to the capital city of the Pāṇḍavas.'

(2)
jā̃́i jaiti patar mā likhyū̃ ca duryodhan kā̃́u ko
to which Jayantī letter in written is Duryodhana of by
'To that capital city the letter is written by the people of Duryodhana.'

he bhula dharmrāj inu kām karyān
O brother Dharmarāja! this work do
'O brother Dharmarāja! do this thing . . .'

pā̃́ci bhai tum cháṭā̃u durpadi lhē ka bhula dharmrāj
all-five brothers you sixth Draupadī taken having brother Dharmarāja!
'you all five brothers along with Draupadī, O Dharmarāja! . . .'

túm hatināpur mā ain
you Hastināpura in come
'You all come to Hastināpura!'

Part III:
(1)
o ho ho báiṭhi caupaṛ báiṭhi caupaṛ ū̃ ki báiṭhi caupaṛ
ϕ ϕ ϕ sat dice sat dicė them of sat dice
'The dice game is set. Their dice game is set'

o báiṭhi caupaṛ, o tu na jai bābu, baiṭhi caupaṛ
ϕ sat dice, ϕ you not go dear, sat dice
'The dice game is set, you don't play! The dice game is set'

kúṭhṛi band kari gain, baiṭhi caupaṛ
room closed done have, sat dice
'They have closed the room. The dice game is set'

ab yū̃ dwī bhayā̃u ki báiṭhi caupaṛ
now these two brothers of sat dice
'Now these two sides' dice game is set'

yo bal kukhēl hū̃d, báiṭhi caupaṛ
this that bad-play is sat dice
'This is a bad play. The dice game is set'

hār jīt ki dwī pá̃suṛi khelala
defeat victory of two pieces play
'They will play two pieces for loss or gain'

Dhol Text 2

Part I	1	2	3	4	5	6	7	8	9	10	11	12	1	2	3	4	5	6	7	8	9	10	11	12
																							G	-
																						↑	tai-	
	G	G	G	-	F	-	FF	C	-	C	-	C	D♭	-	F	-	F	-	F	-	D♭	C	ϕ	ϕ
	di	nā	rā	-	jā	-	dhanu	jai-		bhā	-	ra	to	-	ra	-	yī	-	gyā	-	yā	-	ϕ	ϕ
	Ḅ♭	-	Ḅ♭	D♭	-	C	F	-	D♭	C	C	C	Ḅ♭	Ḅ♭	-	B♭ Ċ	-	C	Ḅ♭	-	C	-	-	-
																			↕		↓			
	bī	-	ra	dha	-	nun	jai-		yī	-	bhā	-	ra	to	-	ra-		yī	gyā-		yā	-	-	-
	-	-	-	-	-	-	-	-	-	-	-	-	-	D♭	-	C	-	C	D♭	F	-	D♭	C	-
													↑											
	-	-	-	-	-	-	-	-	-	-	-	-	-	kā	-	nā	-tha		bha	gū	-	bā	na	-
											D	-	C											
										↑	dwā	-	ri											

1 2 3 4 5 6 7 8 9 10 11 12 1 2 3 4 5 6 7 8 9 10 11 12

B♭ B♭ B♭ C - CD♭F D♭ - φ φ φ B♭ - B♭ C C D♭ F F - D♭ - C

cha la ka pa - ṭa-kai nī- φ φ φ dwā - ri kā nā - rai ṇa - tī - la

B♭ B♭ B♭ C - C D♭ C C - - - - - - - - - - - - - - -

cha la ka pa - ṭa kai ni yā - - - - - - - - - - - - - - -

- - - D♭ - CD♭F - D♭ C C - B♭ B♭ B♭ C C D♭ F - D♭ C φ φ

- - - bha - gō-bā - na - wē - du r ṇā cā ri kā pā - sa - φ φ

C - D

jā - lo

B♭ B♭ B♭ C - D♭ F - D♭ C - C B♭ - C C C B♭ - C C - - -

du r ṇā .jī kā pā sa jā lo drō dha na kā pā . śa yā - - -

1 2 3 4 5 6 7 8 9 10 11 12 1 2 3 4 5 6 7 8 9 10 11 12

\- - - - - - - - - - - -

\- - - - - - - - - - - -

Part II Prose Recitation (rhythm-free):

Bb Bb C D - D C - C C C C - C C ,Bb Bb D - C - C , Bb Bb Bb D - C C C C C C ,

ta bhag - bā - n jī - bun- la gyā̃ - chan ,hē durṇā - cār - yā , hē kap- ṭī - drō dhan bal ,

C - C C Bb C -, Bb - DC C C C , Bb Bb Bb Bb Bb C Db C - C C C C C ,

yē - ṭaim par -, rā - jā ar ju n , da kha ṇa di sa kā - bhār- ta mā bai ṭhyũ ca,

C C D C - C C Bb - Bb A Bb Bb - C C C C C , Bb - Bb Bb C D Bb - Bb

su sṙam dā - nā ka sā - ta mā - ghō - r yuddh chan , yē - bagta mā - bī - r

Bb Bb - Bb Bb C , Bb D - C - C C - C - , C C - C - C C - C -

a bē - ma n ko , i nā - kā - m kā - rā - , kyā la - b$\tilde{\bar{a}}$ - didyā - wā -

Free verse (with previous rhythm) continues:

Language Text of Dhol Text 2

Part I

tai din rāja dhananjai bhārat rái gyāy
that day king Dhananjaya battle remain had
'That day King Arjuna had stayed in a battle'

bīr dhananjai bhārat rái gyāy
brave Dhananjaya battle remain had
'Brave Arjuna had stayed in a battle'

dwā́rika nā́t bhagbān chal kapaṭ kaini
Dwārikā lord God deception fraud did
'God the Lord of Dwārikā! You did deception and fraud'

dwā́rika nāraiṇ tīl chal kapaṭ kaini
Dwārikā Nārāyaṇa! you deception fraud did
'Krishna! You did deception and fraud'

jā́lo bhagbān wē durṇacār ka pās
will-go God that Droṇācārya of close
'Krishna went to Droṇācārya'

durṇa ji ka pās jālo durōdhan ka pās
Droṇa (hon.) of close wil-go Duryodhana of close
'He went to Droṇācārya and Duryodhana'

Part II

bhagbān ji bun lágyā̃ chan
God (hon.) speak beginning are
'Krishna began to speak'

hē droṇācāryā, hē kapṭī drōdhan bal
O Droṇācarya! O cunning Duryodhana! that
'O Droṇācarya and cunning Duryodhana!'

yē ṭaim par rāja arjun dákhaṇ dísa ka bhārat mā baiṭhyū̃ ca
this time at king Arjuna south direction of battle in seated is
'Arjuna is staying in the southern part
in a battle at this time . . .'

susram dāna ka sāt mā ghōr yúddh chan
Susram demon of with in fierce fights are
'He has fierce fights with Susram demon . . .'

yē bagt mā bīr abḗman ka ina kām kāra
this time at brave Abhimanyu of such works do?
'Do such things against Abhimanyu . . .'

kyāla bā̃di dyāwa
Forts bind give
'Set forts'

Dhol Text 3 (no drums)

(1) G - G G G D - F D C - C B♭ G , G - G B♭ C C B♭ C - C B♭ G ,

tai - di na mā myā - ra nā tai - - - - , bhu - lā a - ri ju nai- - - - .

G G B♭ C C B♭ C C C B♭ G , G G G B♭ G C D - C B♭ B♭ - C - - -

bhu lā a - ri ju na rē - - - , da khi na di - śa - - mā pãu chī - yā - - -

- - - - - - - - - - - F - F G - B♭, C - B♭ - C - B♭ C B♭ G , G

- - - - - - - - - - - ka - ba tī - - , kãu - rāũ - kī - - - - - , kā

G G G B♭ D C B♭ - C - C B♭ G , G G C D - - C - B♭ - C - - D

ga li bi lē - khi yā - lī - - - - , ka ba tī - - - kaũ - raũ - na - - kā

C Bb G Bb C D C Bb C - - - - - - - -

ga li bi lē - - khi bhē jyā- - - - - - - - - -

(2) Ab - Bb - C C C C - Bb Ab G, Ab Bb Ab G, , Bb A, - Bb Ab, Ab Ab Ab Ab Bb C - Bb Ab

hē - bō - dā jī ba la - - - -, - -, - -, , yī̃ -, - kā -, ga li pa ri kī - - - -,

G Ab, , C C - Ab Bb Ab Ab Ab - Ab Ab Ab Ab Bb Ab G, Bb Bb Bb C - C C C - C Bb C

- -, mē rō - - - -, mā thō- cam ku nu, ca - - -, a r, bhu jā - ba ba lā - n la gyā̃

- C C Bb - C - C Bb Ab Bb G, , ^G C C C C - C - C C D C C Bb Ab G, , Ab -

- cha na bō - dā - - - - -, - -, , ya dus tāũ kī - kā - ga li a yī̃ ca - - -, , yī̃ -

A♭ - B♭ B♭ A♭ - B♭ B♭ C D C B♭ A♭ G , C - C - C - C - B♭ C - C B♭ C B♭ A♭ B♭
kā - ga li dē - khi ki tāĩ - yī - - - , mē - rī - dā - rī - bu khā - nī cha na - - -

A♭ - A♭ - A♭ - A♭ - A♭ A♭ A♭ - A♭ C B♭ A♭ G A♭ - B♭ C D B♭ B♭ B♮ B♭ B♭ - A♭ A♭
chā - tī - kā - bā - l jaj rā - nā chan - - , mā - thō - - , cam kan , la gyũ - ca bhu

B♭ - B♭ B♭ - B♭ B A♭ - B♭ B♭
jā - bab lā - n la gyã - cha na ,

(3) A♭ - A♭ A♭ B♭ D C B♭ A♭ - A♭ - B♭ C[G] G G G A♭ B♭ C D B♭ A♭ B♭ G - A♭ B♭ A♭ G ,
↑ ā - ja kō - bhā - ra ta - bwā - dā - me rā bã - thā ko - hō - - lō - - - - - ,

Ab - Ab Bb C - D C - Ab Bb C - D C, Ab Bb, C·^{Ab} Ab Ab Ab Bb C D C - C - - - -

ā - ja kō bhā - ra ta - bwā - dā - - -, - -, - me rā bā - thā ko hō - lō - - - -

\- - - - - -

\- - - - - -

Language Text of Dhol Text 3

(1)
tai din mā myāra nātai, bhula arjun
that day on my kin, brother Arjuna
'That day O my kin! O brother Arjuna!'

bhula arjun rē dákhiṇ dísa mā paṹchi ā
brother Arjuna O! south direction in reach ɸ
'Brother Arjuna! Go to the south!'

kabṭi kaṹraũ ki kāgali bi lḗkhi yāli
cunning Kauravas of letter too written have-already
'The cunning Kauravas have written a letter also'

kabṭi kaṹraṹn kāgaḷi bi lḗkhi bhēji ā
cunning Kauravas letter too having-written sent ɸ
'The cunning Kauravas wrote the letter and sent it'

(2)
hē boḍa ji bal yī̃́ kāgaḷi páṛī ki
O uncle (hon.) that this letter read having
'O uncle! having read this letter . . . '

méru mā́thu cámkuṇu ca
my forehead shining is
'My forehead is shining . . . '

ar bhuja bablāṇ lágyā̃ chan
and arms throbbing started are
'and my arms have started throbbing'

ya dustaũ ki kāgaḷi ayī̃ ca
this crooks of letter come is
'This letter of those crooks has come'

yī̃́ kāgaḷi dēkhi kitaĩ méri dáṛi búkhānī chan
this letter seen having my jaws chewing are
'I am eager to destroy them having seen this letter'

chāti ka bāḷ jajrāṇā chan
chest of hair quivering are
'My chest's hair is quivering in excitement'

mátho cámkaṇ lágyū̃ ca
forehead shining started is
'My forehead has started shining'

bhuja bablāṇ lágyā̃ chan
arms throbbing started are
'My arms have started throbbing'

(3)
āj ko bharat bwāḍa méra bā̃ṭha ko holo
today of battle uncle! my share of will-be
'Today's battle belongs to me uncle!'

Repeat

Dhol Text 4 (Prosaic — Non-Musical)

bhagbān ji bunā chan ki āj kāgaḷi áyī̃ ca
God (hon.) saying are that today letter come is
'Krishna is saying that today a letter has come'

arjuna, dáksiṇ dísa mā jāṇ aur
Arjuna! south direction in are-to-go and
'O Arjuna! You are to go in the south'

dáksiṇ dísa mā jaiki susrama ka dānab kā sā́t mā
south direction in having-gone Susramā of demon of with in
'having gone in the south with the demon Susramā . . . '

bhāri ghōr yúddh kan tína
heavy fierce fight are-to-do you
'You are to wage a terrible war'

bhula bhaut satāṇu ca yu susrama dānu
brother! much torturing is this Susramā demon
'Brother! this Susramā demon is torturing us a lot'

bhaut baṛo bhāri ko dānu ca
very big heavy of demon is
'He is a very big terrible demon'

jai dānan bhaut atyācār káryū̃ ca
which demon much atrocity done is
'the demon who has done a lot of atrocities'

magar bhula tu bhārti chai, yúdd karn-waḷu chai,
but brother! you warrior are, fight do-er are
'But brother! You are a warrior, you are a fighter,'

dhans ku calaiya chai aur raṇbhūmi mā jāṇ-waḷu chai
bow of mover are and battlefield in go-er are
'You are a bowman, you are a participant in the battlefield'

magar arjuna twḗ taĩ dáksiṇ dísa mā jā̃n holu
but Arjuna! you to south direction in go will-have
'But Arjuna! You will have to go to the south'

aur dáksiṇ dísa mā twḗ taĩ bhārat kan holu
and south direction in you to war do will-have
'and you will have to do a war in the south'

arjun bunu dida, in kwī́ baṛi bāt nī ca
Arjuna saying brother! as any big thing not is
'Arjuna is saying "Brother! It is not such a big thing . . . '

aur mi susrama dānu ka sā́t mā khud ghōr yúdd karlu
and I Susramā demon of with in self fierce fight will-do
'and I will fight a big war myself with the demon Susramā . . .

aur yúdd karte karte mi susrama dāna taĩ mallu
and fight doing doing I Susramā demon to will-kill
'and I will kill the demon Susrama while fighting . . .

aur bhārat kallu mi
and war will-do I
'and I will wage a war" '

Dhol Text 5

Part I Prose Recitation:

(1) B B♭ - B B B - Ċ - Ċ Ċ B - Ċ - Ċ - Ċ B - , Drumming

a ba - ka ba ṭī - kau - rau n lē - khī - kā - ga ḷī - ,

(2) ^{G}B - Ċ - B Ċ Ċ Ċ Ċ - B - Drumming

jai - tā - mā - bhē jyā lī - - -

(3) B - B♭ B - Ċ - Ċ Ċ Ċ Ċ Ċ B♭ B B♭ B Ċ Ċ Ċ - - - - - - - - - - - -

kau ra ba pār ba ca li gai ni a gad da dē sa pa rā - - - ↕ - - - - - - - - - ↓Drumming

- - - -

(4) Ċ B - B - B - Ċ - Ċ - Ċ B -, , B B - Ċ Ċ B - B Ċ Ċ, , B♭ B♭ B♭ B♭ G,

u nā - kaũ - raũ - na - wē - kū - -, , a bē - ma n kā - bās tā -, , ca ka ra byū-,

- B Ċ - Ċ - - - - - - - -

- rã cā - lē - - - - - - - - -

Part II Drum Pattern Change

1	2	3	4	5	6	1	2	3	4	5	6	1	2	3	4	5	6	1	2	3	4	5	6
G					Ċ	G	G	G	G	-	G	A	G	-	-	-	F	G	F	-	G	-	G
ō					-	me	ri	se	wā	-	ṛi	mā	nī	-	-	-	-	su	ṇī	-	bwē	-	su
G	A	-	-	G	F	D	F	G	G	-	G	A	G	-	G	-	F	D	F	-	G	-	A
ba	da	-	-	-	-	me	ri	se	wā	-	ṛi	mā	nī	-	yō	-	-	su	ṇī	-	wē	-	su
G	G	-	-	-	-	-	-	-	-	-	-												
ba	da	-	-	-	-	-	-	-	-	-	-												

1	2	3	4	5	6	1	2	3	4	5	6	1	2	3	4	5	6	1	2	3	4	5	6
Drumming			G	-	-	G	G	-	A	-	A	A	G	-	-	-	F	G	F	-	G	A	A
			ā	-	-	kaũ	raũ	-	kī	-	kā	ga	lị̄	-	-	-	-	jaĩ	tī	-	paũ	-	chi
A	A	-	-	G	F	F	F	-	G	-	A♭	A♭	A♭	-	G	-	F	F	F	-	G	-	A♭
gau	ya	-	-	-	-	kaũ	raũ	-	ki	-	kā	ga	lị̄	-	ō	-	-	jai	ti	-	paũ	-	chi
A♭	G	-	G	-	F	-	-	-	-			E♭	-	F	G	-	GA♭	A♭	-	A♭	A♭	-	-
gā	yā	-	ō	-	-	-	-	-	-			ar	-	bi	te	-	rō	bō	-	ḍa	yū	-	-
E♭	E♭	F	G	A♭	A♭	B♭	A♭	G	F	E♭	-	F	F	F	G	-	A♭	A♭	-	A♭	-	G	-
nē	ta	ra	-dhwa		ḷ	dā	-	-	-	-	-	a	r	bi	te	-	ru	bō	-	ḍa	-	yū	-

1	2	3	4	5	6	1	2	3	4	5	6	1	2	3	4	5	6	1	2	3	4	5	6
G	-	F	G	G	A♭	A♭	G	G	-	-	-	E♭	F	F	G	-	A♭	A♭	B♭	A♭	A♭	G	G
												↑											
kā	-	rū	-	-	ṇ	ka	r	dā	-	-	-	kā	ga	-	ḷī	-	pa	ṛī	kā	bō	ḍa	ku	-
E	-	F	-	G	-	G	-	A♭	A♭	A♭	-	G	F	F	G	-	A♭	A♭	-	AG	G	-	-
												↓								↕			
ja	-	m̯a	-	pha	-	ti	-	-	ga	ya	-	ka	ga	li	-	-	pa	ri	-	ka	ō	-	-
										↓F	F												
										ga	ḷī												
G	-	F	G	-	F	A	-	G	-	-	-	Drumming											
jā	-	ma	pha-		ṭi	gā	-	yō	-	-	-												

Language Text of Dhol Text 5

Part I

(1)
ab kabti kaṹraũn lḗkhi kāgaḷi
now cunning Kauravas wrote letter
'Now the cunning Kauravas wrote a letter'

(2)
jaĩta mā bhēji yāli
capital in sent have-already
'They have sent it to the capital'

(3)
Kaurab pārb cali gain an̄gad dēs par
Kauravas party gone have-away An̄gada country on
'The Kaurava party has gone away to An̄gada country'

(4)
unā́ kā́uraũn wē ku, abḗman ka bāsta cakar byū́ raci yāli
there Kauravas him for, Abhimanyu for sake circle trap made have-already
'On the other side the Kauravas have set the circular trap for Abhimanyu'

Part II

o méri sewaṛi mā́ni sūṇi bwē subáda
my salutation accept did-hear mother Subhadrā
'My regards to you Mother Subhadrā, Did you hear me?'

Repeat

kā́uraũ ki kāgaḷi jaĩti paṹchi gyāy
Kauravas of letter capital reached has
'The letter of the Kauravas has reached the capital'

arbi téru bōḍa yu nētar dhwaḷda
right-along your uncle this tears drops
'Your uncle at the same time is shedding tears'

arbi téru bōḍa yu kāruṇ kard
right-along your uncle this crying does
'At the same time your uncle is crying'

kāgaḷi páṛī ka jāma phaṭi gāy/gayo
letter read having cloak torn have
'His heart is broken having read the letter'

Repeat

Dhol Text 6 (Prosaic — Non-Musical)

akhīr mā jáb kāgaḷi dharamnáth ka pās mā paṹchi
last at when letter Dharmanātha of near in reached
'At last when the letter reached Yudhisthira'

syām kī ṭaim larkaũ taĩ iskōl ki chuṭṭi mīli
evening of time boys to school of vacation met
'In the evening the boys left their school'

ab apṇa ghauru par āṇ baíṭ gain naúna namān
now own homes on to-come begin have boys all
'Now all the boys have begun to come to their homes'

ab abémanya ka pās mā sandya kī pāṭi bagal par
dharī̃ chai wē ki
now Abhimanyu of near in dusk of writing-board
under-arm on held had him of
'Now Abhimanyu has under his arm the writing board
for the evening'

caldo caldo apṇa tāu ka pās par āye
walking walking own uncle of near on came
'Walking along he came to his uncle'

tāu kā múk najar lagáye abémanyuna
uncle of face glance threw Abhimanyu
'Abhimanyu threw a glance at his uncle's face'

wē ku tāu kyá ca maṇ maṇ kā ā̃́su jyóṇū ca
him of uncle what is maund maund of tears shedding is
'What is his uncle doing? He is shedding very large tears'

Dholki Text 1

1 2 3 4 5 6 7 8 9 10 11 12 13 14 | 1 2 3 4 5 6 7 8 9 10 11 12 13 14

E E E - DC D - C C D C C GA GE G E G - A C CD C D AC C C C CD

ma du so - dhana jī - sa ci tā - nã da - - - tu ma rā - nā ma maca bhalī - - ā nã da bhai-

C D C D E CD CD C C D C C GA GE G E G - A^C - CC D D - ^C A C C C

ma du ma di so dham - - sa ci tā - nã da - - - tu ma rā - nā - mase bha lī - ā nã da bhai-,

Dholki Text 2

F F F E FF FE DE C C D C C GA GE E G G - A C CC - D AG CA C C CD

ma dhu so - dhana jī - - - sa ci tā - nã da - - - tu mā rā - nā ma maca bhalī - - ā - nã da bhaijo

E E E G EED AG CC C C D - A G - A A G E G - AC AC D - CA C C CC CCCD

ma du so - dhana so - dhana saci tā - nã dā - tu mā rā - nā - mase - bha 1̄ - ā nã da bhali ānãda bhai,

Language Text of Dholki Text 1

mádusodhan ji sacitānā̃d, tumára nām ma ca bhali ānā̃d bhai
Madhusūdana (hon.) Being-Consciousness-Bliss, your
name is in good joy brother
'O God! O Lord! In your name is the real joy, brother!'

mádisodhan sacitānā̃d, tumára nām se bhali ānā̃d
madhusūdana Being-Consciousness-Bliss, your name from good
joy
'O God! O Lord! From your name is the real joy'

Language Text of Dholki Text 2

mádhusodhan ji sacitānā̃d, tumára nām ma ca bhali ānā̃d

mádusodhan sacitanā̃nd, tumára nām se bhali ānā̃d

Dholki Text 3

1 2 3 4 5 6 7 8 9 10 11 12 | 1 2 3 4 5 6 7 8 9 10 11 12

C C C - D F D F F F F F | G FD C - C D C B♭ - B♭ D C

ma thu ra - mã raĩ - da pa r bhu jo | bha gi- bā - na jī - - - raĩ da jo

C C B♭ B♭ B♭G B♭ CD F DC C C B♭ | G B♭ - D C - C C C - C C

rā jā - u kra- - sai - na- - bha gi | - bā - na jī - ma thu ra - thu ra

C ma

- D F D F F F G F F (G) - D C | C D C B♭ G B♭C C DC C B♭ B♭ C

- mã raĩ da pa r bhu bha gi- - bā - | na jī - - rãĩ dā- rā jā - u kra sai

D D - F DC B♭ B♭ C - C C - | C - C C C B♭ C C C - D -

- na - par bhu- u kr sai - na jī - | raĩ- da bhai jo - ma thu ra - mã -

1 2 3 4 5 6 7 8 9 10 11 12 | 1 2 3 4 5 6 7 8 9 10 11 12

FD F F F F F F G F^{G}F D C C | DC C B♭ CD DC C D^{D}C B♭ B♭ CD D -

raĩ- da pa r bhu r bhu bha gi- bā - na | jī- - - rāi- da rā -jā u kra sai- nā -

F

pa

F D C B♭ B♭ C - C C G G G | G G G G G B♭ G - B♭ G F F

par bhū - u kra sai - na jī u kra śai | na bhai tai rā ja kī - - cha yī pa r

F F G F D ^{D}C - C - C D C | - ^{D}C G B♭ B♭ - CD D - F D -

bhu jo bha gī - bā - na - cha yī rā | - nī pa ba na - re- khā - par bhu-

DC C C D

bhagi bā na jī

F F F D C CB♭ C ϕ ϕ

pa ba na re - khā- jī ϕ ϕ bha gi bā | - na - - tai rā ja - ki cha yī ϕ

Language Text of Dholki Text 3

máthura ma rā́ida párbhu jo bhagbān ji
Mathura in live lord! who God (hon.)!
'There lives in Mathura, O Lord! who, O God! . . .'

rā́ida jo rāja ugrsain bhagbān ji
live who king Ugrasena God (hon.)
'lives there (who) is king Ugrasena, O God.'

máthura ma rā́ida párbhu bhagbān ji
Mathura in live lord! God (hon.)!
'In Mathura there lives, O Lord! O God! . . .'

rā́ida rāja ugrsain párbhu ugrsain ji rā́ida
live king Ugrasena lord! Ugrasena (hon.) live
'there lives king Ugrasena, O Lord! Ugrasena lives there.'

bhai jo máthura ma rā́ida párbhu bhagbān ji
brother who Mathura in live lord! God (hon.)!
'O brother! In Mathura there lives, O Lord! O God! . . . '

rā́ida rāja ugrsain parbhu ugrsain ji
live king Ugrasena lord! Ugrasena (hon.)
'there lives king Ugrasena, O Lord!.'

ugrsain bhai tai rāja ki chayī párbhu jo bhagbān ji
Ugrasena brother that king of was lord! who God (hon.)!
'Brother! There was that king's, O Lord! O God! . . . '

chayī rāṇi pabanrekha párbhu pabanrekha ji
was queen Pavanarekhā lord! Pavanarekhā (hon.)
'there was the queen Pavanarekhā, O Lord!'

bhagban tai rāja ki chayi [párbhu bhagbān ji
God! that king of was lord God (hon.)!
'O God! That king had a queen, O Lord! O God!'

chayī rāṇi pabanrekha párbhu bhagbān ji
was queen Pavanarekhā lord! God (hon.)!
'there was the queen Pavanarekhā, O Lord! O God!'

bhagbān tai rāja ka chayā párbhu pabanrekha ji
God! that king of were lord! Pavanarekhā (hon.)
'O God! That king's was, O Lord . . . '

chaya apūtar jōg párbhu bhagbān ji
were non-progeny luck lord! God (hon.)!
'was a childless destiny, O Lord! O God!']

Note: We have not provided musical notation for the portion in brackets.

Dholki Text 4

1 2 3 4 5 6 7 8 9 10 11 12 1 2 3 4 5 6 7 8 9 10 11 12

(1) C C - D♭ F - ᴳF F - F F A♭ A♭ B♭ A♭G ᶠᴰC- C C D♭ C ᴮ♭Ċ C C

↑ma thū - rā ma - raĩ da -par bhu - i lō - - nā- raĩ na yā - raĩ da -

C ↓ raĩda

C C - A♭ B♭ C D D C C C D F F A♭G ᴰ♭C - Cᴰ♭ C C C C C C

rā jā - u ga ra sē nā -par bhō - u ga ra- sē- nā jī - na jī bā raī

C - ↑ se -

C C - D C D F D F D C D F F - ᴰ♭C - C C - ϕ C C -

↓ma thu - rā - ma raĩ - da par bhō - a yē - nā - raĩ nā - ϕ raĩ da -

D D ᶜB♭ A♭ B♭ D D C B♭ C C D F F A♭ᴳ D C C - Ċ Ċ Ċ Ċ -

rā jā - u ga ra se nā -par bhō - u gra - se - nā - na jī bhai tū -

Ċ ↑ se

1	2	3	4	5	6	7	8	9	10	11	12	1	2	3	4	5	6	7	8	9	10	11	12
A♭	A♭	-	-	C	-	C	-	D♭	F	A♭	G	D	C	D	F	A♭	G	C	-	C	C	-	ϕ
				↕					↓														
tai	rā	-	- D↓C	rā	-	jā	-	ka	cha	yā	-par		bhō	-	o	yī	-	nā	-	raī̃	ṇā	-	ϕ
				tai																			
C	C	-	D	C	B♭ A♭ (bracketed, dotted)	A♭ (dotted)	B♭ (dotted)	C	D	D	C	C	C	D	F	A	G	D♭ C	-	C	C		
we	ka	-	a	pū	- - (bracketed)	ta-		rā	jō	ga	-	cha	ya	-	a	yī	-	nā	-	raī	ṇā		

Language Text of Dholki Text 4

mát́hura ma r̄áida párbhu ilo n̄araiṇ
Mathura in live lord! hey Nārāyaṇa
'Lord! O Nārāyaṇa. There lives in Mathura,

r̄áida r̄aja ugrsēn párbho ugrsēn ji
live king Ugrasena lord! Ugrasena (hon.)
'There lives in Mathura, O Lord! King Ugrasena, Ugrasena'

b̄arai máthura ma r̄áida párbho
O great! Mathura in live lord!
'O great! There lives in Mathura, O Lord! . . . '

ayē n̄araiṇ r̄áida r̄aja ugrsen párbho
O Nārāyaṇa! live king Ugrasena lord!
'O God! There lives in Mathura King Ugrasena, Lord!'

ugrasena, bhai tu, tai rāja ka chayā parbho oyī nāraiṇ
Ugrasena, brother you, that king of were lord! O! Nārāyaṇa!
'Yes Ugrasena, O you brother! That king's was, O God!'

wē ka apūtar jog chayā ayī n̄araiṇ
him of non-progeny lucks were O Nārāyaṇa!
'That king's was a childless destiny, O God!'

[n̄araiṇ bhai re wē r̄aja ka chayā parbho
Nārāyaṇa! brother O! him king of were lord!
'O 'God! O brother! That king's was, O lord!

da si n̄araiṇ wē ka apūtar jōg chayā ilo n̄arain
lo! that Nārāyaṇa him o non-progeny lucks were hey Nārāyaṇa
'You see! O God! That king's was a childless destiny, O God!'

ab ai n̄araiṇ bhai ik din samai bód pabanrekha ji
now O Nārāyaṇa brother! one day time says Pavanarekhā (hon.)
'Now O God! O brother! one day Pavanarekhā says . . . '

swami khud hwē gī bhauti párbho ilō nārainṇ
lord! urge become has a-lot lord! hey Nārāyaṇa
' "O husband! I am feeling a great urge," O God!']

Note: We have not provided musical notation for the portion in brackets.

Daunr Text 1

(1) D - C C C C - D - C - B♭C B♭ A♭ B♭ A♭ A♭ B♭ - C C - A♭ B♭ A♭ G♭ A♭

o - lak sa da la - kaũ - rãu - kī -, - - -, sa bā -, la gī - gau - yā - yē

B♭ B♭ A♭ B♭ C C - B♭ A♭ C - C - - , C C - C C - C C - - - - - - - - - - - - - - - - - - -

lak sa da la - yē - kaũ-, raũ- kī - - , sa bā - la gī - ga yē - - - - - - - - - - - - - - - - - -

2) D D - D D C B♭ C, C B♭, A♭ B♭ A♭, A♭ B♭ - C C - A♭ B♭ B♭ A[G]

o pā̃ - cā pã dau- -, kī -, - - -, sa ba - la gī̃ - hō - lī -

G A♭ - G A♭ B♭ C C B♭ A♭ B♭, C - D C C - C C C C - C - - - - - - - - - - - - - -

pā̃ - ca pã daũ - -, kī - sa bā - la gi ni hō - lī - - - - - - - - - - - - - -

(3) G - D D D D C, C - B♭ A♭, C B♭, A♭ B♭ A♭, G G G - G A♭ -, A♭ B♭, - A♭ -

ō - lak sa da la -, kaũ - raũ -, la -, - - -, bā rā mā - sa - -, dē -, - ba -

A♭ - B♭ C - C - B♭ - C -, F C, - C C - C - C - C - - - - - - - - - - - - - -

bā - rā mā - sa - ū - nai -, - cā, - lu kai - rī - bhā - rwē - - - - - - - - - - - - - -

(4) D͡G D D D D D E♭ D C, C C C D - D D C B♭, ,

o pā daũ kī khā ta -, rai -, cā lu kai rī - bhā ro - -,

B♭ B♭ C D - B♭ - C - D, ,C C C C D, C - C - - - - - - - - - - -

pā dau ki khā- ta - rai - -, ,cā lu dyā yā -, bhā - rwē - - - - - - - - - - -

Language Text of Daunr Text 1

(1)
o laks daḷ kā́uraũ ki sába lagi gāye
ɸ a-hundred-thousand party Kauravas of assembly started has
'The assembly of many Kauravas has started'

Repeat

(2)
o pā̃c pā́ḍaũ ki sába lágī̃ holi
ɸ five Pāṇḍavas of assembly started will-have
'The assembly of the five Pāṇḍavas must have started'

pā̃c pā́ḍaũ ki sába lagṇī holi
five Pāṇḍavas of assembly starting will-be
'The assembly of the five Pāṇḍavas must be starting'

(3)
o laks daḷ kā́uraũḷ bā́ra mās dēb
ɸ a-hundred-thousand party Kauravas twelve months God!
'Those many Kauravas throughout every year, O Lord! . . . '

bā́ra mās ū́n cā́lu kari bhāṛo
twelve months they moving made deception
'throughout every year they kept deceiving them'

(4)
o pā́ḍaũ ki khātar cā́lu kare bhāṛo
ɸ Pāṇḍavas of sake moving made deception
'They kept deceiving the Pāṇḍavas'

Repeat

(5)
o íbari jo kalla kilaũ ko bhārat
ɸ this-time the-fact-that will-do forts of war
'They will indeed do the war of forts'

íbari rāc yāle kilaũ ko bhārat
this-time plan have-already forts of war
'This time they have already planned the war of forts'

(6)
o koṭu ki laṛai jaṇd arjan
ɸ fort of fight knows Arjuna
'Arjuna knows the war of forts'

Repeat

(7)
hē bhimm arjan kresn utrakhuṇṭ hola
ɸ Bhima Arjuna Kṛṣṇa Uttarākhaṇḍa wil-be
'Bhīma, Arjuna and Krishna must be in Uttarākhaṇḍa'

sósamā ka sā̃t júdd kana hola
Sosamā of with fight doing will-be
'They must be doing war with Sosamā'

(8)
o laks dal kaṹraũl cā́lu kaye bharo̤
ɸ a-hundred-thousand party Kauravas moving did deception
'Many Kauravas started deceiving'

Repeat

(9)
hē kaṹraũ ki kāgaḷi jaiti mā ai gyāye
ɸ Kauravas of letter capital in come has
'The letter from the Kauravas has reached the Capital'

Repeat

(10)
ō kāgaḷi kaṹraũl kya bayān lékhi
ϕ in-the-letter Kauravas what description wrote
'What did the Kauravas write in the letter?'

o kāgaḷi mā ū́n kya bayān lékhi
ϕ letter in they what description wrote
'What did they write in the letter?'

(11)
o sacca pā́ḍau hwelya, ailya pāḍapō
ϕ true Pāṇḍavas will-be, will-come Pāṇḍavas!
'You will come if you are true Pāṇḍavas, O Pāṇḍavas!'

ailya pāḍapo kilaũ ka bhārat
will-come Pāṇḍavas forts of war
'You will come to the war of forts, Pāṇḍavas!'

(12)
o kũti māta ka hwēlya dhirgpāl
ϕ Kuntī mother of will-be braves
'You must be the brave ones of your mother Kuntī'

pā̃c pā́ḍaũ hwēlya dhirgpāl
five Pāṇḍavas will-be braves
'The five Pāṇḍavas must be brave'

Daunr Text 2

Part I

```
A C A - C A - - - - - ,A - C C - C E - D E - D E D - - - -
↑ā - - - - - - - - - - ,ā - ja ba - dai nu - hwe yī -rai jai nā - - - -

A - C - - - - - - - - - - - - - - - - - - - - - - - - - -
          ↕      ↓
yē - - - - - - - - - - - - - - - - - - - - - - - - - - -
                                                 A - - - C,
                                                ↑hē - - - yē,

C - A - C - D E - E - D E A - C - ,A C A C D - D D - -
↑
hwē - yī - jai - nā san - tā - nī -, rē - - - ,au -, - -, lā - da yē - -

- - - - - - - - - - - - C - E - E D C D - E - D - C - D -
↕         ↓
- - - - - - - - - - - - ↑ba - san - tā - nī rē - au - lā - dai - - -
               G⌒D
              ↑
               o  ja
```

```
C A C - - - - - - - - - - - - - - - - - C ,C - A - C - C D A
  .                                          .           .
          ↕         ↓                  ↑
ai - - - - -  - - - - -  - - - - - - - - ,hō - lā - - - pan da pa
                                                        .   .
                               A - - -
                              ↑.
                               hē - - -

C D E - D - E - D A - C D - D - - - - - - - - -
                  .
                                     ↕                  Drumming
a ba jaĩ - tī - kā - re - - - bā - rai- - - - - - - - - -


Part II

G⌒E D - E - E D D C A ,C D E - D D - C A C - - - C - - - -
                    .                  .
                        ~                              ↕
o ja ba - jaĩ - tī - ī - - ,mā ja la - ga lī - ī - - - - - - ai - - - -


C - - - - - - - - - - - D E - D - E - D - D C A C D - - - - - - - -
                                              .
      ↓                ↑                       ↕                 Drumming
yē - - - - - - - - - - - ki bā - rā - dau - rī - kī - - sa bā - - - - - - - -
                                             .
             A - C
            ↑.
             pan - daũ
              .     .
```

Language Text of Daunr Text 2

Part I

(1)

ā̃ ā jab dáiṇu hwē rē jain yē
ϕ ϕ when gracious become ϕ may ϕ
'When God may be come gracious'

hē yē hwē jain santāni rē aulād yē
ϕ ϕ become may worthy-to-be-born ϕ progeny ϕ
'May there be born a worthy progeny'

o jab santāni rē aulād hē hola
ϕ when worthy-to-be-born ϕ progeny ϕ will-be
'There are the worthy sons . . . '

paṇḍap ab jaĩti ka rē bārai
Pāṇḍavas now capital of ϕ about
'The Pāṇḍavas now in the capital'

Part II

(2)

o jab jaĩti mā̃j lagli páṇḍāu ki bára dauṛi ki sába
ϕ when capital in will-start Pāṇḍavas of twelve round of assembly
'When the big court of the Pāṇḍavas will take place'

Hurki Text 1

Part I

A C D E♭ - - E E♭ D C C C - C C - C C - C A C C C C C

jai - - - - - gu rū - a ṛ dā - s kā - m dā - s sa t pu ri ā s

C - C - D D - E♭ D C - C C C C - C - C - C C C ᴬC - C C - C -

jē - tē - tu mā - rē - nā - m l̃ē tu mā - rē - nā - m lē ke bhū - ke nā - w̃ē -

C C C - C C C - C C ᴬC C C - C - D D - E♭ D C C C C C C - C ᴬC - C -

jim me - ga yē dū - dū tē chu ṭi j̃ā - w̃ē - ba hō - - - ta l bē kam mā - s khā - ū̃ -

C C C - C C C C - C - C C - C - C C - C - C D E - E C B B♭ A A♭ G

par ṇ pā - ū̃ isul lā - sā - brat jī - kwī - ni jā - wē - ja - lla - kē pi yās- - - -

Drumming

Part II

A G A G G E D C D - E♭ D A C C - D A C E D E - D C C - C C - D - - - -

o bā ba bi nō tī - khu nā - - - lai - yī - rē - - gā yā rē - - - bī - r bā - bā - - - -

C D - A A C A C A C C - - - - - | Drumming | A G A E D C - C D D E♭ D

a yē - yā - - - - - - - - - - - | - - - - - - - - - - | o jan ni ghū -, rā̃ dū bī rai - -

C C C D E E D E - D D - A A A - A - ᶜA - B♭ C - - - - - - -

tan ni wē ku pa ra can dai - rū pai - - hwē gā - yā - bā- bā - - - - - - -

Drumming - Singing

Part III

1 2 3 4 5 6 | 1 2 3 4 5 6 | 1 2 3 4 5 6 | 1 2 3 4 5 6

A - - G A - | Ċ - Ċ G - ED | C - - CA - - | A - C D D -

ō - - tyō ro - | pa - r can - da | rū - - pā - - | hwē - gi bai rā -

1	2	3	4	5	6	1	2	3	4	5	6	1	2	3	4	5	6	1	2	3	4	5	6
D	-	-	D	C	A	D	-	E	G	-	A	D	C	-	D	-	-	A	-	C	D	D	-
yē	-	-	yē	yā	-	pa	-	r	can	-	da	rū	-	-	pā	-	-	hwē	-	gi	daũ	dya	-
D	-	-	C	A	A	D	-	E	G	-	A	D	C	-	D	-	-	A	-	C	D	D	-
yē	-	-	yē	yā	-	pa	-	r	can	-	da	rū	-	-	pā	-	-	hwē	-	gi	daũ	dya	-
D	-	-	C	A	A	G	A	-	G	G	-	D	-	C	C	A	A	A	C	-	C	-	D
yē	-	-	yā	-	ō	tyō	rū	-	mē	rī	-	pā	-	-	rū	-	-	ba	tī	-	a	-	ba
D	-	-	C	A	-	D	-	E	G	-	A	G^A	-	-	G	E	-	A	-	C	Drumming - Singing		
yē	-	-	yā	-	-	sau	-	-	ma	-	-	na	-	-	hī̃	-	-	dō	-	lu			
															Ċ	Ċ	-	-	Ċ				
														↓	ā	dē	-	-	s				

Language Text of Hurki Text 1

Part I

jai guru aṛdās kāmdās sat pūri ās
victory teacher praise Kāmadāsa certain full hope
'Victory to Saint Kāmadāsa whose praise certainly fulfills the wish of those

jētē tumārē nām lẽ tumārē nam lēkē bhūke na ā̃wẽ
whoever your name take your name having-taken hungry not come
'Whoever utters your name, by your name nobody remains hungry'

jam mē gayē dūt dūt tē chuti jāwẽ
Yama in went messenger messenger from be-left out
'Those gone to Death are freed from each (of Death's) messenger'

bahotal bekam mās khā̃ũ

ɸ ɸ ɸ ɸ

parṇ pā̃ũ isulla sābrat ji kwí ni jāwe
life regain Isulla Sābrat (hon.) any not goes
'May I regain life. None of the devotees like Isulla and Sābrat go to death.

jal kē piyās
water of thirst
ɸ ɸ ɸ

Part II
o bāba biṇoti khún lai rē gyāy rē bīr bāba a yē ā
ɸ monk seed-package open begin ɸ has ɸ brave monk ɸ ɸ ɸ
'The brave monk has begun to open the seed package'

o jánni ghurā̃du bīr tánni wēku parcaṇḍ rup hwē gyāy bāba
ɸ as swings brave so-on his fierce form become has monk
'Just as the brave monk swings the package
his form becomes fierce'

Part III

o tyóru parcaṇḍ rūp hwē gi bairagi yē yē yā
ɸ your fierce form become has renunciate ɸ ɸ ɸ
'O renunciate! Your form has become fierce'

parcaṇḍ rūp hwē gi ḍaũḍya yē yē yā
fierce form become has Ḍaũḍyā ɸ ɸ ɸ
'O Ḍaũḍyā! Your form has become fierce'

Repeat

tyóru méri pārbati ab yē yā sau maṇ hĩḍolu
your my Parvatī now ɸ ɸ hundred maund cradle
'O my Pārvatī! Yours is now a cradle weighing 100 maunds'

ādēs
instruction
' ɸ '

Hurki Text 2

F ^D F F F G F F - D C - ,C C D F, F G F - G - - - - - - - - - - - - - -

tu dai ni hwa yī ja yī - mā tā - ,du ra - -, gā bha wā - nyā - - - - - - - - - - - - - -

A A -

tu dai -

G F Ab G - G - G - Ab - G F, F G - D - D F G - Ab G F D F, D F F - F

ni hwē jā - - mā - tā - mē - rī -, sa ka - la - bha wā nī - me rī - - - jō ga mā - yā

- - - - - - - - - - - - - - - - - - - F - Ab G F D, D D, D F - G F, G

- - - - - - - - - - - - - - - - - - mā - tā - - -, te ro, ja la - ma -, nō

G A, F F G G

hē -, kā̃ tē kā̃ tē

- F - G - G Ab G F, F

- hō - yē - te rū - -, ja

D Ab - Ab - G -

pai lē - ma - tā -

A♭ - G F D F F D F G A♭ G - F D F D F F - - - - - - - - - - - - - -

lā - - - - kō ā - sa na me rī - - - - - - mā tā - - - - - ↕ - - - ↓ - - - - -

- - - - - - - - G - G - F - A♭ G F D, D D F F G G - F G - - - -

- - - - - - - - ↑ nī - ca -thal - lā - - -, ū pa ri ni a gā - sā - - - - - -

G F F -

↑

to jal lā -

- - - - - - - - - - - - - - - - Ċ A♭ G - A♭ G - A♭ G F - F F G F

↕ - - - ↓ - - - - - - - - - - - - ↑ nī ca - - mā tā - ta khā - - gi ri nī -

Ċ Ċ Ċ Ċ Ċ

↑

mē ru mandi ra

F D D D F - G - A♭ - G F ^{D}F D F F - F - - - - - - - - - - - - -

ca - ka bi lā - sā - mē - rī - - jō ga mā - yā - - - - ↕ - - - - - - - - - - - -

```
- - - - - - - G F F Eb Eb - D C -, C C - C D F F G Ab G G - F G
- - - - - - - ↑ yā - kā ra mā - ga - -,hwa yī - jal lā -thal lā - - bhū - myā -
    G F F G Ab
  ↑
    hē wē jal lā -

- - - - - - - - - - - - - - - - - - - - Ċ Ċ Ċ Ab G F G - G - Ab
      ↕       ↓
- - - - - - - - - - - - - - - - - - - - ↑ ga r mã - - - mā - tā - pai
                    Ċ Ċ Ċ Ċ
                    ↑
                    tai ja l sā

- G F -, F G Ab G F D - F F - G Ab G Ab - G F D - DF - - - - - -
- lī - -, nā da - - pai - - dā hō - yē - - mē - rī - mā - yā - ↕ - - - - -

- - - - - - - - -
↓ - - - - - - - - -
```

Language Text of Hurki Text 2

tu daíṇi hwē jai māta durga bhawāni
you kind become may mother Durgā Bhavānī
'Mother Durgā Bhavānī! May you become kind!'

tu daíṇi hwē ja māta méri sakal bhawāni méri jog māya
you kind become do mother my all Bhavānī my Yoga Māyā
'You please be kind, my Mother! O all-pervading Bhāvanī,
my Yoga Māyā!'

hē kā̃ te kā̃ te māta téro jalmaṇo hōye
ϕ where from where from mother your birth became
'Where were you born Mother!'

paíli māta téru jāl ko āsaṇ méri māta
first mother your water of seat my mother
'O my Mother! Was water your seat first?'

to jal ní ca thal upari ni agās
then water not is land above not sky
'Well there was neither water nor land nor sky above!'

méru mandir ní ca māta ták giri ní ca kabilās méri jog māya
my temple not is mother there mount not is Kailāsa
my yoga Māyā
'There was no temple of mine, nor Mount Kailāsa,
O my Yoga Māyā!'

hē wē jalākār mā̃ga hwē jal thal bhūmi
ϕ that watery-form out-of became water land ground
'Out of that watery form came out the ground with water and land'

tai jal sāgar mā māta páili nād paida hōye méri māya
that water sea in mother first sound born was my Māyā
'O my Mother, the Māyā! First sound was born in that sea'

A *ghasyari* Song Text

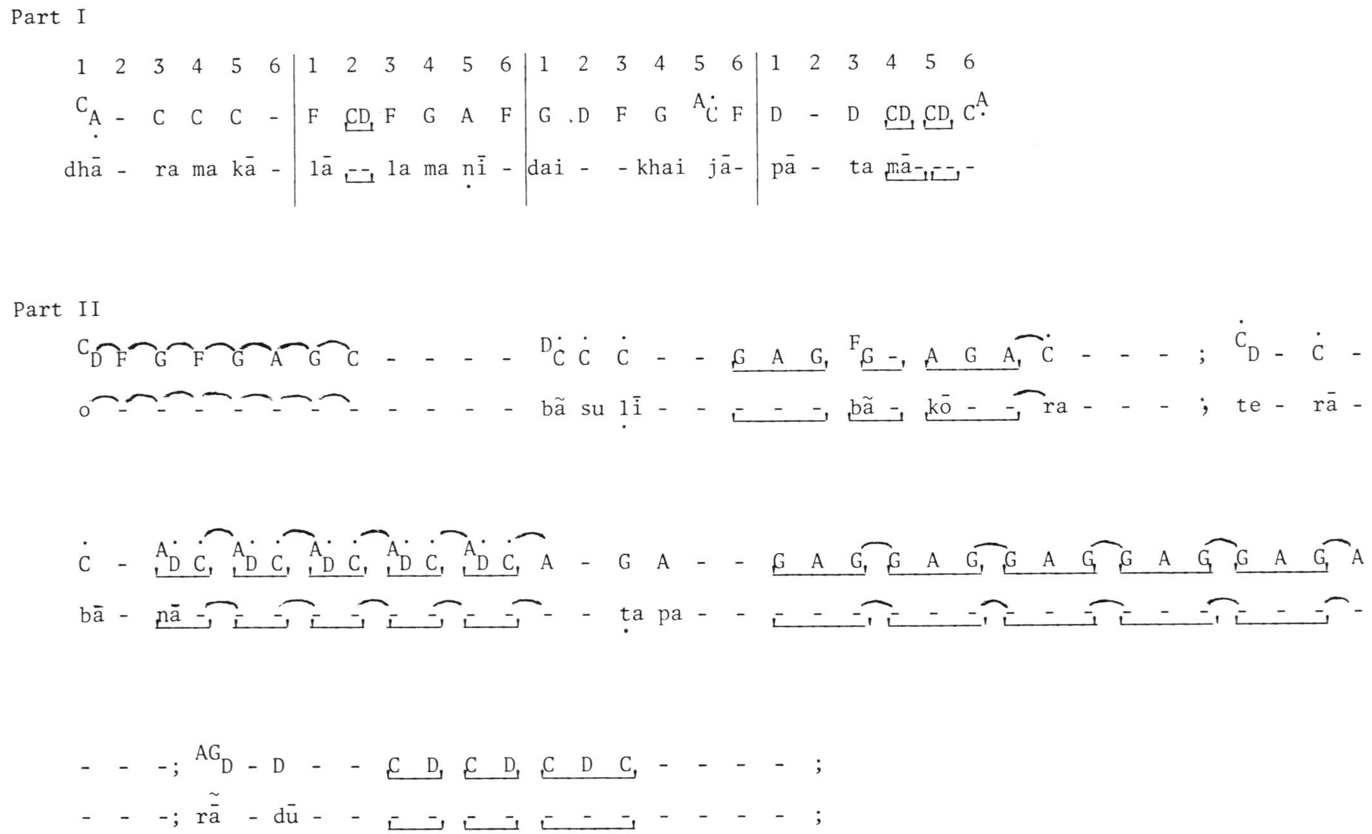

Part III

1	2	3	4	5	6	1	2	3	4	5	6	1	2	3	4	5	6	1	2	3	4	5	6
Ạ^{C}	-	C	C	C	-	F	CD	F	G	A	F	G	D	F	G	^{A}C	F	D	-	D	CD	CD	C^{A}
ḍā̃	-	ḍa	si	ca	-	kō	--	ra	ma	ṇī	-	dai	-	-	khai	jā	-	pā	-	ta	mā-	--	-

Language Text of the ghasyari Song Text

These stanzas are from a folk song taken from the collection of Keshav Anuragi. The musical notation has also been provided by him. The other stanzas of the song, including (3a) and (3b), are arranged musically like (2a) and (2b). This popular love song pictures a young highland girl (a reaper who cuts and gathers grass) looking for her lover Lāl Maṇi in the mountains. The song is therefore called the '*ghasyari gīṭ*' 'grasscutter's song' (or 'Reaper Song').

(1)
dhār ma ka lāl maṇi! dái khai ja pāt ma!
saddle on of Lāl Maṇi! curd eat go leaf in
'O Lal Mani of the mountain saddle! Come, eat curd on a leaf'

(2a)
ō bāsuḷī bākōr
Ⓞ flute's bamboo
'Bamboo of the flute . . . '

(2b)
téra bāna ṭaprādu ḍaḍā si cakōr
your sake glance-around hill's like *cakor*
'(I) look around like the *cakor* bird on the hill'

Repeat

(3a)
o rósni cirāg
0 light lamp
'Light and lamp . . . . '

(3b)
rāt rāt din din mi téri phirāg
night night day day I your search
'Every night and day I search for you'

Repeat

Mãgaḷ Text

The *mãgal* songs are auspicious in nature. They are sung on the occasion of a joyful *saṁskāra* ceremony such as a marriage, a naming ceremony, an ear-piercing, the first haircut of a male child, etc. The Dhol-Damau drumming may or may not occur with these songs. The singers are usually women, and are never the Dhol-Damau drummers themselves.

The following song text is sung at the time of the sacred bath which is given to the bride before her wedding. A stanza of this song can be repeated. Although all stanzas have an ideally identical musical composition, no two stanzas have exactly the same tones and beats. Since there are usually two or more singers the tones and beats of each singer will vary slightly from that of the other participants.

The following two stanzas are the first two stanzas from one of the song texts recorded in our field work.

m̃āngal Text

(1) G G - B♭ B♭ - B♭ B♭ - B♭ B♭ - B♭ - B♭ G B♭ - C - D C - -
nyū ti - lā wā - nyū ti - lā wā - ba - ru bā - - ma - na yē - -

B♭ C - C - D B♭ B♭ B♭ - G B♭.C - D C - -
jai na - dē - na ha la dī - kā b̃ā - da yē - -

(2) G G - B♭ B♭ - B♭ B♭ - B♭ B♭ - B♭ - B♭ - G B♭.C - D C - -
nyū ti - lā wā - nyū ti - lā wā - m̃ā - ji - kā gē - na yē - -

B♭ C - C D - B♭ B♭ - B♭ - G B♭.C - - D C - -
dē lī - m̃ā jī - da ī - dū - da b̃ā - - da yē - -

Language Text of the mā̃gaḷ Text

(1)

nyūti lāwa nyūtī lāwa baṛu bámaṇ yē jain dēṇ haldi ka bā̃d
having-invited bring having-invited bring great brahmin ɸ
who has-to-give turmeric of bā̃d
'Welcome, welcome to the great priest who will give the
turmeric *bā̃d** (to the bride)!'

(2)

nyūti lāwa nyūtī lāwa mā̃ ji ka gēṇa yē
having-invited bring having-invited bring mother (hon.)
of jewels ɸ
'Welcome, welcome to the jewelry of the mother!'

dēli mā̃ ji dái dū̃dā bā̃d yē
will-give mother (hon.) curd milk's bā̃d ɸ
'Mother will give (to the bride) the bā̃d of curd and milk'

*Just before the bath the bride goes through a ceremony called *bā̃d* (or *bān*) *dēṇu* 'to give *bā̃d*'. In this ceremony, first the priest and then every woman present (starting with the bride's mother and excluding widows) places a paste on the toes, knees, shoulders and head of the bride, who is sitting on a small stool under a canopy. The paste is made of turmeric, gram flour, etc., and is considered sacred. Then it is applied to her entire body by one or more women. Thus the paste functions as a mask as well as making the body soft and shiny.

BIBLIOGRAPHY

Austerlitz, Robert. 1966. "Text and music in Mansi songs." *Current Musicology*. Spring 37-57.

———. 1967. "Two Giliyak song-texts." *To Honor Roman Jakobsen. Essays on the Occasion of His Seventieth Birthday*. 99-113. The Hague: Mouton.

Berreman, Gerald D. 1963. *Hindus of the Himalayas*. Berkeley and Los Angeles: University of California Press.

Bhatkande, V.N. *Hindusthānī Sangīt Paddhati*, 6 Vols. Series in Marathi. Bombay: B.S.Sukhtankar (Hindi translation from Sangeet Karyalaya, Hathras).
1920. Vol. 1.
1921. Vol. 2.
1922. Vol. 3.
1923. Vol. 4.
1937. Vol. 5.
1937. Vol. 6.

Bloch, Bernard and George L. Trager. 1942. *Outline of Linguistic Analysis*. Baltimore: Linguistic Society of America.

Bloomfield, Leonard. 1933. *Language*. New York: Holt.

Bright, William. 1963. "Language and music: areas for cooperation." *Ethnomusicology*. 7:26-32.

Chandola, Anoop C. 1956. *Garhwālī Bhāṣā* ('The Garhwali Language' in Hindi). Unpublished Thesis for the Master's degree in Hindi. Lucknow University.

______. 1963. "Animal commands of Garhwali and their linguistic implications." *Word*. 19: 203-207.

______. 1966. *A Syntactic Sketch of Garhwali* (University of Chicago Ph.D. dissertation in Linguistics). Ann Arbor: University Microfilms.

______. 1969. "Metalinguistic structure of Indian drumming: a study of musicolinguistics." *Language and Style*. 2: 288-295.

______. 1970. "Some systems of musical scales and linguistic principles." *Semiotica*. 2: 135-150.

______. 1973. "On the Stress Behavior in Musicolinguistics." Chicago: *Proceedings of IX International Congress of Anthropological and Ethnological Sciences*.

______. 1975. "An evolutionary approach to sentence formation." *Linguistics*. 150: 15-46.

Chao, Yuen Ren. 1956. "Tone, intonation, singsong, chanting, recitative, tonal composition, and atonal composition in Chinese." *For Roman Jakobsen. Essays on the Occasion of His Sixtieth Birthday*. 52-59. The Hague: Mouton.

Chatterjee, S. K. 1926. *The Origin and Development of the Bengali Language*. Calcutta: Calcutta University Press.

Chomsky, Noam. 1957. *Syntactic Structures*. The Hague: Mouton.

______. 1965. *Aspects of the Theory of Syntax*. Cambridge: MIT Press.

Grierson, George A. 1916. *Linguistic Survey of India*. Vol. IX. Part IV. Calcutta: Superintendent of Government Printing.

Harris, Zellig S. 1951. *Methods in Structural Linguistics*. Chicago: University of Chicago Press.

______. 1957. "Co-occurrence and transformation in syntactic structure." *Language*. 33: 283-340.

Herzog, George. 1945. "Drum-signalling in a West African tribe." *Word*. 1: 217-38.

Hockett, Charles F. 1958. *A Course in Modern Linguistics*. New York: Macmillan.

Jairazbhoy, N.A. and A.W.Stone. 1963. "Intonation in present-day North Indian classical music." *Bulletin of the School of Oriental and African Studies*. 26: 119-132.

Lamb, Sydney M. 1966. "Prolegomena to a theory of phonology." *Language*. 42: 536-573.

Mahar, J. Michael (ed.). 1972. *The Untouchables in Contemporary India*. Tucson: University of Arizona Press.

Majumdar, D. N. 1944. *The Fortunes of Primitive Tribes*. Lucknow: Universal Publishers.

Merriam, Alan P. 1964. *The Anthropology of Music*. Evanston: Northwestern University Press.

Morgan, Kenneth W. 1953. *The Religion of the Hindus*. New York: The Ronald Press Company.

Nettl, Bruno. 1958. "Some linguistic approaches to musical analysis." *Journal of the International Folk Music Council*. 10:37-41.

Pike, Kenneth Lee. 1947. *Phonemics, A Technique for Reducing Languages to Writing*. Ann Arbor: University of Michigan Press.

Rajagopalachari, C. 1950. *Mahabharata*. New Delhi: The Hindustan Times.

Raturi, Hari Krishna. 1928. *Garhwāl kā Itihās* ('History of Garhwal' in Hindi). Dehradun: Garhwali Press.

Sankrityayan, Rahul. 1958. *Kumāū̃* ('Kumaon' in Hindi). Banaras: Jan Mandal.

Seashore, Carl E. 1938. *Psychology of Music*. New York: McGraw-Hill.

Singer, Milton. 1972. *When a Great Tradition Modernizes*. New York: Praeger.

Springer, George P. 1956. "Language and music: parallels and divergencies." *For Roman Jakobsen. Essays on the Occasion of His Sixtieth Birthday*. 504-513. The Hague: Mouton.

Turner, R. L. 1931. *A Comparative and Etymological Dictionary of the Nepali Language*. London: Kegan Paul.

Wood, Alexander. 1944. *The Physics of Music*. London: Methuen.